VIA Folios 144

A Space Between

A Space Between

Anna Citrino

BORDIGHERA PRESS

Cover photo by Michael Citrino

Library of Congress Control Number: 2019943151

Printed in the United States.

Published by
BORDIGHERA PRESS
John D. Calandra Italian American Institute
25 West 43rd Street, 17th Floor
New York, NY 10036

VIA Folios 144
ISBN 978-1-59954-149-5

CONTENTS

I. Origins

II. *Il Strano Paese* • The Strange Country

III. History

IV. Starting Again

V. Another Generation

For Michael Citrino, and for those who have left their homes.

*One doesn't discover new lands
without consenting to lose sight of the shore
for a very long time.*

ANDRE GIDE

I. Origins

SOUTHERN ITALY

White salt shoes. Hard citrine body.
The sun strides through the dry hills and dusty
oaks behind Amantea and San Lucido.

Heat sizzles the village streets. Light hauls
its weight from stone to stone, sinks into walls.
The sun's great eye opens and defines

house, goat, wheat, chaff, sea, wealth
and poverty. The sun lifts its sword to cut
day from dark, carves destinies with its gaze.

Here, messages come on bird wings.
Through the shapes of clouds, angels
might appear. The soil you planted in is dust?

A picture has fallen from the wall? Beware
the evil eye. Scatter salt at the door to chase
away the fear. Do you long for softness,

a gentle breeze, some respite? Open your eyes.
In this world there is only so much goodness.
To give to one means to take from another.

LUISA'S STORY

I was a spinner in those days, a weaver. Spin and turn, turn and spin,
thread passing through my fingers, falling at my feet like the years

my mother waited for my father to come home, not knowing
what happened. Days passed, as cholera, malaria, and starvation

consumed the village. I continued on, spinning wool and silk
as mama taught me, hoping someone would be left for me to marry.

My longing pooled with the yarn in baskets at my feet, waiting
to be woven, until mama and the tailor who bought her cloth

stitched together a plan for his son to meet me, and Alberico arrived.
His name means king of elves, though people called him by his

second name, Gaetano. I led my brothers through San Lucido's
village streets into Gaetano's barbershop one morning where

he waited, door open. Room scrubbed clean, air scented with soap,
rinsed with sun, the boys' stubborn cowlicks and stray hairs

disappeared under Gaetano's confident hand, their dark tufts
falling like feathers to the floor. Our faces mirrored with smile.

It wasn't too late for my life to change. My name means
famous in battle. A name given to strengthen me for struggle,

but with Tano I felt at peace. At San Lucido's saint day *festa*
we danced the tarantella and celebrated our engagement.

Spinning, turning, his feet bobbed, bounced with energy. Alive!
His eyes shone as I wound under his arm. Our parents smiled,

and our weaving began. We married. Our first son,
Cosimo, arrived and became our world.

I walked the hills, searching for food. Gaetano cut hair.
Thread by thread, we clung to life.

Evenings, we'd carry Cosimo down to the sea, water rippling
against the shore. We gazed out at the lapping surf, its tongue

telling stories of another world we could enter.
Dreams are dangerous, but Tano began to talk of crossing

the ocean, going to America. "Swim in it," he suggested,
splashing gleefully. "See how it feels."

Women didn't do that—tradition, and too many clothes.
We went down, though, secretly, one August midnight,

and I slipped into the Tyrrhenian while Tano held Cosimo
standing on the shore. I waved my hands through the water,

kicked my feet, leapt up, and let the sea hold me.
Peering into the starry night, I leaned back.

On shore, Gaetano lifted Cosimo into the sky—white salt stars
spilled across blue night. Cosimo's small hand reached

for the starlight's sputtering spray. Heat rising from the stony street,
we walked home, Tano twirling, singing some silly song.

When we arrived, we fell on our bed laughing, bodies wet
with happiness, ready to sail anywhere.

THE CUT
Gaetano's Fear

When Garibaldi rid Calabria of the French,
my parents celebrated with the countryside.
But no leader stood up for us, so, the mafia
filled the gap, and we continued on,
choked by the Camorra's control.

I knew San Lucido's faces.
Antonio Mazza, San Lucido's Camorra man,
had an angular face with a sharp personality.
Mazza despised his father, beat his wife, carried a knife,
and looked for an excuse to use it.

"Haircut," Mazza said standing in my barbershop doorway.
His sour voice squeezed the air from the room
as he twisted his body into the barber's chair,
raked his fingers through his shock of hair,
and splintered me with his eye.

"Make me look good," he snapped,
showing me his knife point. He was a short man
who wanted to look more than he was.
I got out the scissors. "You're a working man, Gaetano."
I didn't speak. I knew what he wanted.

The smell of baking bread drifted down
from our upstairs apartment. Cosimo. Luisa.
We needed everything we made.
How could I give anything to Mazza?
"Your father got this shop for you.

Isn't that right?" I held the scissors, ready to cut.
Mazza rubbed together his forefinger and thumb.
"Everyone visits your shop."

I stared at Mazza's neck, the blood pulsing
beneath his skin. My hands sensed heat.

I grabbed a chunk of his hair, gave it a whack.
Mazza jumped from his seat, his body a wound spring.

"You pay me now!" he demanded.
"I gave you your cut," I said.
Mazza spun. His blade splintered the air,
flashed at my throat. "You're young," he said.
"You want this business?" He spit the words.
"Want your moon-faced wife?"
He smashed a bottle against the wall,
cleared a shelf with one swipe. Razors,
combs, tweezers, toilet water, shaving mug
clattered to the floor. He shoved me against the counter,
his voice venom. "Want your Cosimo,
your one year old?"

Mazza pressed his yellow teeth and onion breath
into me. "You pay!" In our apartment upstairs,
I heard Luisa call to Cosimo. I grabbed Mazza's wrist,
my arm trembling under his weight.
Wet with sweat, my hand slipped.
His blade cut my collar.

"You pay what I ask," he bellowed, his words
erupting into the street. Sammarro, the town guard,
burst through the doorway, seized Mazza's arm,
fought him for the knife.
Mazza exploded. Furious. His blade
stabbed and carved the air, reaching for flesh.
I called into the street for help.
Six men bolted into the room. Together,
we held Mazza as Sammarro wrestled the knife
from Mazza's grip.

Arrested, hands behind his back,
Sammarro prepared to drag Mazza away.
Eyes slashing the air between us,
hair wild and wet with sweat, Mazza turned to me,
"I will remember you," he promised,
chin thrust up defiantly. His words
sliced the afternoon light, fell into my chest,

a dark lock on the floor
waiting to be swept away.

LUISA EXPLAINS HOW IT HAPPENED

The birds had stopped singing, and gulls
from the sea below circled overhead
as I pumped water from the well for laundry,
pounded clothes against stones, trying to scrub
Mazza's words to Tano "I will remember you,"
from my thoughts, but they remained—
a stain in our home's fabric that couldn't be removed.

When the town guard denounced Mazza,
the mayor made him undertaker
to appease Mazza's resentment—
an undertaker from the underworld.

Like before, I cooked, cleaned,
sewed, and sang to Cosimo,
but a shadow followed me,
and the fear of shadows,
as if the earth had been cut open,
ghosts let loose.

I thought of Mazza's wife, the loneliness
that roamed the rooms inside her house's stony walls,
sea spanning below her window, but her,
stuck inside, boats and harbor beyond sight.

Caught inside summer's choking sun,
I bent over a stone sink, rinsing a shirt,
swirling water across my arms and hands
to cool myself, Cosimo resting
beside me in a basket.

Up the street I heard shouts.
A door slammed.
Mazza burst onto the walkway,

stomped toward his house,
blade glint in his hand.

Dropping the wet shirt I held,
I threw a dry cloth on top the basket
where Cosimo lay to hide his face,
then ran to tell Tano.

He shut the shop.
We scrambled to our house upstairs,
locked the door, and waited inside.

Later, as we sat at dinner,
Mazza roared from the stairwell.
"Open up! I killed, Samarro,
and I want you."

His blows pounded against the door.
Tano's eyes locked with mine.
Silently, we reached for each other's hands.
"Gaetano!" he yelled, kicking the door.

Cosimo cried, his wails a siren
hurtled against the walls. I lifted him to me.
"I'm here," I soothed.

"Are you going to cower with your baby
or do you have the courage to come out?"

The door shuddered.

Tano scurried to a cabinet across the room,
and dragged it toward the door, legs screeching.
I set Cosimo at the table,
and ran to help heave the furniture
in front of the door.

Behind me, Cosimo squirmed in his chair.
Plates clattered to the floor and shattered.
A quick turn, a leap from his seat.
A fall, and a cry cut short.
Hands lifeless. Neck broke.

Tano and I vaulted to Cosimo's side.
Mazza's shouts piercing our ears like nails,
his thunder reverberating off the stairwell wall,
we bent over Cosimo, watched
as his eyelids fluttered,
then closed.

A butterfly,
his breath floated out into the room,
light as the stars.

Lighter.

Sun sinking outside the door,
I curled him into me.
Gaetano's arms surrounding us,
we leaned against the wall,
night swallowing us
in canyons of darkness and broken rock.

THE WAY IT WAS
Gaetano's Prayer

At night, mosquitoes buzz in the darkness. Everywhere,
something waits. North, our landlords clink their coins,

while here in the south, we work the land: cracked hands
cleave the earth, carve sparse gardens between hard stone and sun.

Silently, the hawk circles above, wind against wings
as we walk to St. Francis of Paola's shrine—Cosenza's patron saint,

Calabria's. Ours. St. Francis was a poor man. He would've understood
our plea. *Calabrese* dance, yes, feet stamping, bodies turning.

We dance to shake off death, to stay alive. Dancing
is not enough now, though. Last week, my child died.

Cosimo curled beside us, soft cheeks, small voice—
gone. Our spark of everything. His absence an emptiness

wider than the world, deep as the distances of endless space.
Nothing is big enough to hold this grief.

Mother of the broken-hearted, we come to you. Knees
against stones. We kneel before you, give you our mountain

of sorrow. Is it true, there's only so much good on earth, that evil
must balance out the good received?

I'm but a barber, Luisa a weaver. How can we live?
Give us a sign. Make us whole.

GAETANO'S DREAM

Last night, I dreamed of bees, two bees dead
on a black mound or nearly—like Luisa and me

since Cosimo died. I had a net, a small scoop of gauze
fastened to a stick I put under their bodies.

I lifted them, and they rose, flew away.
This morning, bees fill our room. I drive them out,

but more appear. Eating, sleeping, the bees flow in.
Where they come from, I don't know. Legs heavy

with yellow pollen, the bees hide in the corners.
Like others before, they want to push us out—make our house

their hive. We've given up chasing them now.
We fall asleep to wings buzzing above our heads, the whole room

whirs and whispers, as if the room itself is ready to fly.
"It's a sign," I tell Luisa, "Time to leave Calabria, make a new home."

LUISA ALONE

This afternoon Gaetano left for the *strano paese*,
along with his cousin. The train shrinking from sight

in a black roar. He said he'd send for me. Arms empty,
I wait in San Lucido, with Mama once again,

waiting as she waited. She loved her Alessandro,
as I love Tano. Why couldn't Papa come

back to her—to us? The wind blows.
The grass on the hills dries.

Fog climbs the cliffs below the village,
seeps into the corners and chinks.

On it goes, thread after thread the weaving.
What will come of my life, I don't know.

I hold my questions
the way trees hold birds—

I let them come.
I let them go.

LUISA CONSIDERS THE FUTURE

Seven years ago, I married the man whose face
I now gaze at in the photo his cousin brings from California.
Tano, a man whose eyes are dark rooms
where I once lived and rested
while I spun the fabric we wore and he shaped stories,
light stretching from the sky in wide sheets to our clothes
drying on the line, quietly folding warmth into the weft and weave.

But how do I tell about the way the world crumbled
when our baby died and Tano left with his cousin
for America? How to describe the plains of light
that keep falling, as if to dry out the sea itself
and turn the world to stinging salt?
Some days I could walk all the way to San Francisco.
Instead, I do the chores that keep me spinning.

When Tano's cousin returned, he told about the quake
he survived in San Francisco, the thousands homeless.
But now, here, too, in Calabria, the earth has ruptured.
A hundred thousand dead, maybe two—who knows
how to count the scar of loss?

First the quake's rumble, a rattling throng of cracking vibration.
Furniture, plaster, walls—centuries of civilization collapsed.
Buildings toppled and broke, crushed families
under stone and brick. Dust choked all
in a suffocating pall. Then the sea rose
a raving, sickled wave. A Mt. Etna of water
wiping the world away in one swift blow.

Now, thousands upon thousands wander homeless,
straggle in to San Lucido from Reggio and Messina
like scared, abandoned dogs circling through scree-filled streets—
vacant-eyed, looking for any hollow wide enough to rest in.

The world has perished,
but we continue on.

We dream of more,
we find less.

When I married, I wanted a home, a child.
I got an empty chair and broken threads.
The castle on the hill atop our town
has cracked and tumbled.
It will never be rebuilt.
We make our lives the way the earth does.
Things shift, fall apart, then continue on.

Sometimes the sea below town is turquoise,
sometimes purple. My lungs contract,
expand with the color. We have nothing,
yet the sky is still with us.

I rave against the sea's ranting waves
and shattered shores but it has already
laid down to rest, attentively licking
the paws of it coastline, its breath falling,
rising in gentle waves. Amidst uncertainty,
rest can still be found.

The rooms of Tano's eyes are distant and dark,
but their door is still open.
There is depth in darkness.
There is shelter.

When I go to him, I'll make those rooms my home.

LUISA'S WORLD

So many winters have passed, nights stretching into days. Quietly,
I twist the threads and turn the spindle, make it spin—strands

flowing endlessly through my fingers, like the days and hours
I wait to hear from my husband while threads expand into fabric

for shirts and skirts, vests. "I'll send for you," Gaetano promised
nearly a decade ago. I remind myself of his face in the sunrise's

clear light when we first married, his face's sturdy lines,
his mouth's perfect curve, his chin's strength, and remember

the way he turned again at the train's window at the last moment,
his eyes' dark depths—a country I belonged in,

even as the train took him from me. Going to America
to find a new life was a good plan—the promise of work

he'd heard of in San Francisco, something beyond
the circling wheel we were born into.

The quake broke San Lucido's wheel. It could take a lifetime
before it'd spin again. Now, I too will go.

"It's a little like Calabria," returning villagers tell me,
"but more people, buildings, traffic." I've longed for the moment

I'll be with him—have buried my face in the clothes he left behind
to find his body's faint scent still present. Years have trudged by

while we've saved money so I can join him. California
will have changed Tano. The years apart will have made us strangers.

Fear is part of life, but I choose to ignore it.
So many men had left Calabria before Gaetano and I married.

He could've chosen another woman, but he and his family chose
me. I can stand on my own, but I still want him. I'm going.

Gaetano sends word, "Outside the city the grassy hills shine golden
in summer." He sees them from above Telegraph Hill. I try

picturing them, but mostly I see the Sila mountains behind
San Lucido covered in pine and scattered with goats, heads bent

grazing on grass. "Other *calabrese* will be there, too, Luisa—
a village inside the city," my sister Agnetta reminds me.

"They speak our language, make our food." There's a grief
in going, though—not just the uncertainties of leaving alone,

the three week's ride stuffed in a ship hold without air,
or my questions about what life with Gaetano will be like

after a decade apart, though all these will be hard enough.
It's the little things that make and hold this world I'll miss—

Mama's hands, and the brown bowl she makes pasta from,
how Agnetta's face opens into a smile, June's Battista *festa*

with music rolling down the street, the seagull's call above
the steep shore, the grassy hills behind town sending out

their perfume when it rains, the stone step leading to our door.
I know happiness doesn't depend on any of these things.

Across the water, Tano prepares a place for me, a thread
of moonlight strung across the sea. Love is greater

than anything I could leave behind in this small town,
but this evening, the church bells ringing into the crisp night air,

the whole world seems found and lost in their call
rippling like the rising tide through October's streets.

II. *Il Strano Paese* • The Strange Country

GAETANO'S ARRIVAL

Some people stay. Some people leave.
I was one who left.

Bread starter in the purse, garden seeds, and hard salami,
a handful of lira, an extra shirt: at Ellis Island, *L'Isola delle Lacrime*,
this is what many carried to start their new lives.

The many men leaving San Lucido for America
had clipped away my customers, shaved my life
to bare skin, until I too felt forced to find a different life.
I didn't go to Mulberry Street like other *calabrese*.
The boat ride over was cramped enough.
Could've stayed with relatives in New Jersey
or gone to Brazil or Argentina with some of my cousins.
But I'm not a farmer.
Plantation work isn't right for me. I have a skill.

I wanted to live in San Francisco's hills near the Pacific—
thought they'd make me feel at home.
Though most Italians there were northerners
who didn't speak my dialect, I didn't want to meet
another *camorristi* in New York or New Jersey whose knife
could again cut away my world. San Francisco was farther away,
smaller. Less trouble there, I thought.
So, after Ellis Island, I sailed on
round the Tierra del Fuego, encased in the boat's ribs,
praying that in California I'd be free.

Spewed out into the city like Jonah from the whale,
I was a new man.

I started work right away cutting hair
in North Beach for people from Genoa,
Naples, Calabria. A familiar life, but cut new

with a different shape.
This world is not the cramped shoe life
of San Lucido. I can save money,
work towards a shop of my own
make a place for Luisa to come to.

Every day, I'm cutting hair for vegetable sellers,
laborers, fishermen, listening to their stories—
how the peach harvest has begun, a wall been built,
or fish been hauled in—small stories,

knots in a net holding the world together one day to the next.
People like the trim, new shape I give their hair,
the way I can make their rough edges fall
to the floor, forgotten, ready to be swept away.

Work is good, but work is not all.
I don't want my story to be only about what can be cut.

A year now, Luisa and I've been apart.
Every night, when the moon rolls up from the horizon
or the dark pushes into the street, I want her—
her round hips and smooth body,
my woman of pearl, her dark hair tumbling across my chest,
a waterfall or ocean,

but she is not with me.

My bed has become the boat I sailed here on—
a hard rack of dreams choked with desire,
stinking with sweat—every inch crazed
with parched hope.

The *Mezzogiorno* with its citron perfumed orchards,
and ox heart tomatoes in hillside gardens—
though I gave them little attention, these grew

in the heated land I came from.
Luisa continues on in that world
with its thorns and entangling vines,
tasting, still, its bitter sweetness.
This city has no place for them.

Here in San Francisco's fog-choked world,
I need Calabria's blue air, the weight
of water curling beside me
to make it clear
how to hold on to her
while still letting go.

THE OTHER ISLE OF TEARS

She can't write, but she sends messages—
a blanket or a shirt a cousin carries across the ocean
to remember her by,
though these come years between.

I keep them, thinking of her hands that made them,
how her love follows me across the years
while, like an olive tree, she continues on,
slowly growing while waiting for water.

Luisa knows the world is hard.
You can't change fate.
When her father left, he never returned.
Eventually, word came that he'd died,
and her mother found another man.

Before he was a tailor, my father was a carpenter
who knew how to build a strong house.
As a child, I watched him form a foundation,
raise a wall, frame a window and a door for the family.

I thought I had done that with Luisa when we married—
that we'd built a house nothing could shake apart.
I've not died like Luisa's father, but the man who vowed
to give himself to Luisa alone
has left.

I'm a practical man, I try,
but I'm not good at carpentry.
Like my father, I've changed.
That's not enough to explain
why I let Vincenzina's smile interrupt
the life I'm working toward with Luisa.

Sometimes I go to listen to Sid LeProtti play piano
at the So Different Café, but the waiter girls
on the Barbary Coast's Pacific Street are known to drug
their customers so others can club and rob them blind.
Brothels and dance halls—you can be shanghaied there.

At the boardinghouse, though, I watched Vincenzina
roll the shells for cannoli. Her hands light, quick,
her voice a spark as she offered me *dolci*.
She ground chocolate for pastries, filled them
with meat and almonds, made everything sweet.

"Have this granita al caffe," she suggested,
her eyes steady. "Dark, smooth, strong.
You'll like it."

Better than her cannoli, better than loneliness,
the ladles of her tenderness—her body's texture
stirred into mine. More than once, she brought me
her dessert, and I didn't turn her away.

Luisa will be grieved.

You can't clip a vow free
as if it were a lock of hair. Hair grows back.
It's not the same with vows or the trust they're made from.
Some things should never be cut,
but I can't change what is.

Love endures beyond loss,
Luisa and I learned that when our Cosimo died.
I need Luisa's steadiness, her strength,
like I need bread.

Ellis isn't the only Isle of Tears.
I'm standing on an island now I can't turn back from.

I've broken away from the mainland.
All I can do is find a boat to sail onward,
and hope to find a way
to make a home again.

GAETANO LEARNS FROM A STRANGER

A throbbing, guttural rumble wrenched from earth's rocky depths
broke open that morning, and yanked me from bed. The house
creaked and bent, then jolted from its foundation in a boom.

I grabbed my trousers, called to my cousin, and dashed out the door
to see the street bed buckle, and buildings rattle, ripple and sway
before plunging to the pavement—brick and stone toppled

atop each other in gigantic ruin. Dust clouds rose into the sky.
The land trembled and shook in periodic spasms. We walked
out to the main road, stepping across tumbled brick and twisted

streetcar tracks to stare across the city as the sun rose,
revealing everywhere, buildings that had collapsed—
homes, businesses, warehouses, all demolished in a destruction

worse than war. We walked until we came to the hill
above the Presidio, then sat in silence, watching a wall of fire
shoot flames into the heavens as it cut across the city, spreading

its smoky veil, turning the sky strangely orange. The blaze
raged for days, leaving half the city homeless. Tens of thousands
went without water for weeks. No food to be found.

I wasn't alone. It wasn't only the newcomers who had it hard.
Rich and poor built street sheds, and slept in the parks.
People cooked on brick ovens they made in their yards.

I got food at the Presidio, and helped clear the streets of rubble.
Everyone worked together to restore, rebuild—there was plenty to do.
The first days after the quake, I remember all those people

wandering the streets, trudging along, bundles slung over
their shoulders or drug behind them on a board, women
hauling their babies, men huddled together on the street,

stupefied as voices called out from beneath beams and rubble,
the pavement pulsing in aftershock before another wall
gave way. The world had broken open. I stood there

with the masses in that wilderness without words,
the earth rocking beneath my feet, cinders burning
in the choked air, and watched a man, his shoulders

wracked in tremors like the earth itself, wailing
for his lost wife and child. We're all refugees, I realized.
Everyone's life is broken. What did anyone have

to carry them out of bedlam but family?
"I'm going back to Italy," my cousin told me.
"Carry a message," I asked. "Tell Luisa to come."

There was a city to be built. A life. They need us.
I wasn't afraid of what was hard. Neither was she.
Together we could make a life.

GAETANO OBSERVES

I live by the Pacific. One season, all is well. The next,
water swells, clouds grow, storms ride in.

Everything turns. When I landed in San Francisco in 1899,
the first automobile rolled down Van Ness Avenue.

Next year, the Bubonic plague struck Chinatown,
followed by riots and barbed wire blockades.

That passed, and I rejoiced with thousands of others
walking the concourse at Golden Gate Park

for the Spreckels Temple of Music dedication.
Five months later, the City of Rio de Janeiro steamer

hit rocks, and sank at the bay's entrance, Italians
with their fishing boats, rescuing survivors.

Last year, Hawaii sent San Francisco the first
electronic message across the ocean through cable wires,

and electric trolleys rambled south to San Mateo. A bigger
curiosity is Mayor Schmitz and his lawyer friend, Ruef,

receiving payoffs from everyone in the city, and how
the railroad companies are California's Camorra—

a brotherhood of bosses who manipulate politicians.
Cooks, waiters, longshoremen, carriage makers, butchers,

packers, clerks, telephone and streetcar operators
went on strike in 1901. Politicians want to keep their cash,

control and corruption. Like Calabria's *camorristi*,
violence, a code of solidarity, and silence chokes us

while those in power call their actions honorable.
I didn't run from Calabria to California hunting for wealth

like those a few decades before me who came in a rush,
deserting their boats the moment they arrived

to head for the hills and look for glimmers of gold
they could grab overnight. I came to make a life.

Italy is a new idea, only a few decades old.
Americans call us Italians, but we identify with our regions,

our cities. Most in San Francisco are *genovese, lucchese,
ligure,* citizens of Tuscany—northerners. I'm from Calabria.

The south. I speak, and they know I'm not one of them.
Like chemicals used to curl or bleach the hair,

they shape and color me into a look they've identified
as poor, unschooled, superstitious, and stubborn.

The world tries to tell me who I am. When I arrived,
my language, clothes, history, my very skin were wrong,

but I don't accept what others tell me I am or have to be
just to keep my business in order. The world I'm making

isn't only for myself. I have the future to think of.
In San Lucido, the *camorristi* would've pursued me

for defying them. But San Francisco, too, constricts
my choices. I know what and who I am—

an everyday man. A barber.
A man in a world of limited options

with little to hold on to, and the little I have
can be cut away.

I comb through the hair of the short years I've lived,
and know the choices I have are thin.

I'm part of a workers' union that tells me goals
I should strike for. But I know what I want—

a shop of my own, family to come home to,
Luisa's arms around me, her food on my plate—

a simple dream, but big for a man like me,
and opportunity enough.

Calabrese believe to take from one side
always means another must be given to,

everything balanced out.
I visit Molinari's, and select a salami

to share with my cousin. As family,
as *calabresi*, we hold together

but there must be a path between extremes
to make a life and find a home. I'll learn them.

Last day of March. Today marks twenty-three days
of rain. The world floods with water and change.

LUISA LEAVES HOME

Footsteps on the hard cobble last twilight—
harsh echoes that clattered through the brain

while I sat at the window, listening
to a child calling "Papa, papa,"
from a window above as his father

wended his way up the steep hill from the sea,
coming home from work.

Wind pushes the walls, and I unlatch
the door to narrow streets, barren hills
sloping abruptly into sea.

It is morning now,
and I am leaving this life's empty cupboards,

going out of the stony house, the sun's
lemon heat, the salted fish,

out from the familiar rooms and names, out
of all I know.

Down to the water, light rising
on the last day from the white shoreline
as it greets the ocean's immensity, I go.

Slowly, the boat pulls from shore,
the hull breaking open the vast
expanse. From the sky's broken
window, birds cry.

Father, mother, a silent photograph
held in my palm,

I lean forward over the stern,
into the rain,
and cutting wind.

BECOMING NEW

Twisted walls and tracks, houses with gaping gaps—
when I arrived, four years after the quake much had been repaired,

but much was left to do. Half of San Francisco had lost their homes.
Boats brought brick. People scrounged for lumber. Forests fell.

Supplies to rebuild were short, but the whole city was busy
remaking life, not just us.

Maybe when the world falls apart it's a beginning of life,
not the end. That's the way it was for Gaetano and me.

We'd been apart so long. Much had changed.
Like the city, we too were starting over.

After the quake, Mr. Giannini at the Bank of Italy
set up business in the streets, and gave Tano a loan—

trusted his character, he said. That's what I had to do too.
To get to our house the day I arrived in San Francisco,

we had to step over a ditch in the street. Tano reached for my hand,
and I felt mine in his, sure and steady.

That night, past images of ruptured streets and homes,
the strange smells and scenery sifting down into the cracks

of years apart, broken yet alive, our arms trembling
in fear and wonder, we held each other.

The moon's searchlight falling across our faces,
we tethered ourselves to each other's voices,

let its light bind us together, let our bodies carry us
from the collapsed buildings of our past into a new world.

GAETANO AT WORK

Customers. That is what I have. Every day
they come to me, rough-faced, shaggy,
and I lather their faces, share the day
with conversation, and cut away the ragged edges.
I go along, opening the door,
singing as the days grow shorter.

Steep hills and Amantea's interminable sea.
I think of them now, the fields I walked through
outside of town in morning's dim light,
past naked children crying from inside straw
huts with earthen floors. My village was full
of those who bent over broken earth all day,
then trudged home to a crowded
room with a cramped, sweaty bed, everyone
huddled together in the suffocating dark.

My oldest brothers were doctors, but I was the youngest.
Nothing left for me but the barber shop—everything
fixed. Whole villages were filled only with women and children
the elderly. I counted the steps from home, "One, two, three, four—"
and prayed for change, "Holy Mary, Mother of God,
be with us now and at the hour of our death," my blood
running in circles, trying to get out.

Then Luisa spun her way into my life,
her close-knit sweaters, the warm meadow
of her smile. A new world opened.
Half of Calabria had run away, their steps
echoed on deserted streets—why not us?

My mother—her broken face the day I left.
My silence, a thorn piercing the dusty air's heart.
Her eyes, a sea of grief I sailed away on.
Others could shear sheep, but I could shear hair—

and I opened shop.
Luisa followed,
then the war.
But I kept cutting,
and today my second shop opens.
One, two, three, four, I count the men
waiting at the door, though elsewhere
men wait in line for bread.

Three children, now. The more I cut,
the more I have. Gold hills, gold sun
running through the window.
I live in the Golden State.

LUISA DESCRIBES A FAMILY CELEBRATION

I'd given birth to baby number five. Eight months later we visited
the Pan Pacific International Exposition. Tano wore his suit,

I, my blouse with ruffled collar. Baby in arms, the other children
following along, we set off to see the displays—a steam locomotive,

a telephone line linking to New York, and the Liberty Bell brought
by train from Philadelphia. We explored the Italian pavilion, its murals

arches and piazzas, rambled through its gateways and gardens.
Tano splashed the children with water from the Fountain of Energy

as they dashed away laughing. Kaleidoscopic color danced in the azure
sky from the Tower of Jewels covered with 100,000 glass gems.

When evening arrived, searchlights surged from the Tower in pulsating
red beams, reaching across the darkness as if to hold us in its heart.

Like a diamond or a pearl, a new world was opening before us,
old irritations soothed over in scintillating beauty.

We'd left the old world of stone and wood, earthquakes,
and hunger. Despite the grief we'd known, the loss we left,

we knew, at least for the moment, light bursting through the dark,
we'd been reborn into the right country, right city, right time.

MAKING A LIFE

In San Lucido I spun linen, silk and wool—thread sliding
through my fingers season after season
as I stared out at the sea's horizon, wondering
how I could twist together my life's frayed,
thin threads into something bigger than summer's
white sun and winter's cold, narrow room.

We've made a life here together, Gaetano and I,
loss, and hope, wound together in a garment of fog
that rolls in from across the Pacific. I walk through
my neighborhood, a thimble full of narrow streets—
a world no bigger than before but strange. Chinese,
Germans, Spaniards, Greeks, we are loose threads
dangling beneath this country's clattering loom
of tongues, pale faces and pale ways, trying to see
how we might find our way into its fabric.

Gaetano has his barber's shop, but I've given up
weaving. That was my other life. The children
are my weaving now—their lives binding this world
to the one we came from, their eyes, the rosary beads
I pray through, reinventing the world in America.

Arduino and Giovanni wait at the window
in the other room. I knead the bread, stir the soup.
Soon, Gaetano will arrive, his footsteps echoing
outside the door. All day he cuts hair, a little here,
more there, massages the scalp a bit, a splash
of cologne to go—our lives hang on thin strands of hair.

We're not city people, though we're living in one.
We miss our villages' gold walls, the thousand
colors of blue swirling like music across the sea and sky.

We don't know opera, but when Luisa Tetrazzini sang

at the corner of Market and Kearney on Christmas Eve
soon after I arrived in America, we joined the throng.

She sang "The Last Rose of Summer," her white dress
glowing amidst the flood of dark coats and hats.

Clear, pure, her voice floated and danced on wings
above all two hundred fifty thousand of us standing in the crowd
that December night, clinging to its flame.

It lifted us from the bare dirt floors of our past, the longing
for the worlds we'd left behind, and let us believe
that fire and dreams are stronger than iron—
have substance equal to earth.

LUISA'S CIRCLE

Babies, I wanted them, of course, but what I love
is the way he holds me—his arms, like tree branches

nestling me in the shade of his strength, his joy.
During the day, the children's feet clatter through the house.

They wrestle, call, cry. Tano listens to their stories.
He makes them laugh—races the boys down the street,

bounces Chiara on his knee. But he wants his quiet too.
No whining allowed. Like a spun coin that flips

or a sprung spring, he catapults over the wall of calm,
sends the children scrambling across the room. *Rispetto*.

There are lines you don't cross. Irish, German, Armenian—
each neighborhood has its ways, and we Italians have ours.

Their streets. Ours. So many worlds to walk between.
Sometimes, the children straggling behind, I climb the hill

above the city, stretch my eyes across the bay to the world beyond,
remembering my mother bent over earth's open hills

outside San Lucido, looking for fennel, bells clinking
from goats' necks as they grazed nearby. I long for that earth.

We had the village and the countryside to roam.
We owned nothing, but the world was ours to walk.

Here in America, it doesn't matter that you're a *calabrese*,
genovese, or *napoletano*, like it would in our home village.

To Americans, we're all Italian. Tano and I can't see the future,
but we have enough bread for today, and a bit more, too—

clothes, rooms to sleep in. The children, even Chiara,
have school. It's required.

Out there on the streets, Tano has to know
which lines he's crossing.

When he holds me, though, it's all a circle.
There are no lines. We're at home.

GAETANO'S VIEW OF PROTECTION

With five *bambini* and a wife to care for, I've cut more
than corners to own my barber shops. I saved for years

to bring Luisa from Calabria. Worked hard after the quake
when people needed an extra hand to help rebuild. This city

is home now. I don't need any papers to become American,
didn't want to crouch in a trench during the War to prove it.

Luisa, the children, they needed me more
than the government. I've got friends, attend mass.

I don't want to pay any protection people. The men
keep coming by asking for their dues. Sure, I'm Italian,

and every Italian doing business owes them. You can't stand
alone, but those guys are crooks—gun running loan sharks,

gambling on the money they take from me to run their business.
They're the ones I need protection from.

When Schmitz was mayor, boss Ruef demanded bribes from businesses.
Now that Ruef is in jail and Rolph is mayor, the new crime kings,

the McDonough brothers, run the police department with bribes.
The bosses crave their cut.

 "One way or another, you'll pay," my cousin Amadeo reminds me.
"It may be America, but earthquakes come. Storms.

You need protection." It might be prohibition, but San Francisco
isn't dry. Irish, German, *genovese* or *calabrese*, for us, alcohol

isn't evil. Back in 1906, Italians helped put out the Great Fire
with the wine they'd made in their basements.

The government disregards its own rules, though.
Prisons fill with those who drink while gangsters gain

from politicians who want their alcohol. Politicians' power—
it's a big show. They buy people like objects, play them

for what they can get or get away with.
Mayor Rolph invents stories for the press, makes money

from the prostitution house he owns.
I've given what I've had to to keep the business going.

My second shop on Market Street is doing well.
The bosses don't like it. I pay the rent,

but they want more. Prohibition has made them
greedy. Things aren't simple.

I don't need to be handed a *Mano Nera* letter
from the Black Hand to feel the threat of harm.

I don't fit with the Irish, can't compete with the bail bond king,
McDonnough, his police and politician friends.

I'm not blind. Winds rising off the ocean can turn.
Gangsters might chase me down, wait for me

in some hidden hole, but I'm creating a future
for my children. Call me a hard-headed

testa dura calabrese, but isn't this America?
I came to work. Let me do it.

Life is hard.
In Italy, our firstborn fell from a chair and died.

Every healthy man suffers. Food, family, home.
I'm not asking more than this for the work I do.

I'm a barber. I know what to cut and where.
Let me have what's mine.

I stuff today's earnings in my pocket, shut the shop,
step into the damp and dark. It's December 5,

St. Nicholas eve. Nicholas, he knew about protection.
He was a real Godfather. He dropped those sacks of gold

down the chimney for that family so the parents
wouldn't have to sell their children into slavery.

I'll stop at the Shamrock Saloon like I was asked,
have a drink. Got to keep friends on every side.

DECEMBER
Arduino's Discovery

The whole world turned blacker than midnight
that night, the sky stretching far into the torn edge
of infinity as I ran through the streets looking for him,
first at the *taverna*, then the shop
before I saw him lying there in the empty lot
like a piece of crumpled carpet—
my papa,
his iron body broken, bleeding,
head pressed into the dirt.

"Arduino," he said, his breath ragged,
his mouth opening into the darkest
hole as I knelt beside him, "*Casa*."

And I took him home to mama
as he asked. It was too late
for a doctor, too far.

His battered body hefted across my shoulder,
we stumbled and staggered through the streets
to stand trembling and broken at our door, the bruises
on his face giant blue roses opening,
their terrible blossoms swollen with dark blood.

Mama held ice to them, sat by him the rest of the night,
his hand resting on her lap, as he mumbled,
groaned, then fell unconscious. But she went on

whispering "Gaetano, Tano," his name
a prayer. Her lips moving inaudibly, she rocked,
her arms wrapped around her waist.

Dark hair pulled from place

fell in shadowed pools around her shoulders.
She lifted her face, her bright eyes
vacant as she gazed at the rivulets
slipping down the window pane.
I looked at her face, pale
and open as the moon
in an empty universe.

"He's dead, Mama. Dead," I choked it out
into the silence.

My body shuddered.
She inhaled sharply, her hand
fumbling for mine. "All for the money
in his pocket. My papa, our future, gone
because someone else wants a few dollars,
and me, only sixteen."

She pulled me to her and held me.
Neither of us spoke.

From the darkness of the other room
where the children slept

someone cried.

We stood there, alone,
shivering in morning's hollow light,
the last survivors on an island
that had been washed over by a vast
and powerful wave,
left with nothing
but the wind
and the distant, howling sea.

III. History

I.

It could be a story that started like storybooks do—
far away in another time, in the land of Homer's Scylla
beside Calabria's turquoise waters
and humble St. Francis of Paola's home—

a world of crumbling castles and feudal states
where foreign powers and the privileged
wrung the earth for the wealth it could give them,
lived the *calabrese contadini*, the peasants.

This is a story of generations of lives
bent close to the stony earth, histories written
in the rugged land if you have the eyes to read,
if you lean close enough to hear.

II.

An ancient region of ancient people, before the Greeks arrived
and called the land Italy, the Oenotrian vine cultivator tribe
made the southern peninsula their home.

Sun and storms lashing the sea and mountains
along with successive invasions—the Brutti, Romans, Visigoths,
Byzantines, Saracens, Normans, Swabians, Angevins, Aragonese,
Spanish, Austrians, French, and Bourbons—power lengthened
the longitude of its arms' shadow.

For centuries, amidst the swarm of dialects, ancient laws
and the tangled complications of kinships and friendships
weighted with the warren of social obligation, negligence,
decrees, and graft—Italian city-states feuded—
one bloody uprising after the other,

until a thousand red shirts glowing as they marched,
and a million lives later in 1877,
Garibaldi unified the peninsula.

Across the boot, from the Tyrrhenian to the Aegean,
Garibaldi raised Calabria's hopes.

But that didn't make life better for the *calabrese*.
Calabria had no coal, no iron ore, nothing

to create factories to bring them
money like the north.

What did Calabria have?

Droughts, deforestation, and erosion,
overpopulation, near-starvation, illiteracy,

unemployment, and the parasite
that ate the grapevines.

Then, as if Job's plagues had visited the region,
cholera came, and malaria—all these

were Calabria's possessions.

This wasn't the end though.
In 1900, Mt. Vesuvius decided to stir her caldera.

For 35 years, she hurled
her tantrum of hot ash and lava,
violence and fumes

accompanied by the 1908 Sicilian earthquake's
tidal wave that carried off 150,000 people.

What good can rise from loss?

What does longing bring?
People call them stubborn, the *testa dura calabrese*,

hard-headed people living on the hard earth.

Stubbornly dancing the tarantella,
stamping their feet,

and swinging their bodies
they staved off death.

They danced, and created
the dream of a better world.

III.

Maybe their loss was a curse,
maybe a call to adventure,

but southern Italians were used to escaping to foreign cities
when times got hard, leaving behind
education and their families.
Many left to slake their thirst
for survival, laboring

as coal miners, construction or railroad workers
in foreign worlds.

They built skyscrapers, formed streets and made shoes.
Replenished and renewed,

they returned home to their Gulias and Adrianas,
to their sun-scorched hills and village beds,

returned to their hard, stubborn lives,

and carried on.

IV.

But some didn't return.

Between 1880 and 1920,
four million sailed on

to a new world called America

with their simple satchels,
a letter from a relative or friend

calling them to come,
a pebble from their hometown left in their pocket.

And they stayed.

V.

To a world of bed bugs, rats,
falling plaster, frozen pipes,
and dark one-room tenements,
they came.

To a world of America for Americans, gaining names
like "wop," "dago," and "guinea"
with their not quite white skin,

their foreign dialects and strange foods—
their gnocchi, roasted chestnuts,
meatballs, and *limoncello*,

their loud voices, overflowing gestures,
and old world traditions they came.

They stuffed peaches in tins
at the Del Monte cannery,
worked in textile mills assembling collars to coats.
They dumped coal cars, poured molten metal,
and tended blast ovens at steel mills.
They set up banks, sold groceries, and created vineyards.

A garden patch of personalities—
some solid as melons, others malleable as eggplant,
some fiery chilies—each with their stories,
each sending roots into American soil.

But Americans found their food odd,
their festivals troubling—

the way they carried wooden saints
through the streets, and paraded icons

through neighborhoods like pagans.
Too excessive. Strange.

How much new can a person bear
before the world he knows breaks?

So, fear strolled off for a walk with the media.

"Al Capone, Broccolo, and Lanza,
these were mafia men.

Why not dress the Italians
in mafia jackets for easy identification?"
said the media.

"Flat characters for a simpler story
makes the world easier to understand."

Fear agreed.

But there were other stories too—

Rosa Ponselle singing to the crowds,
Eddie Lang's guitar melodies, and Venuti's violin,
Valentino's presence on the silent screens,
the Piccirilli brothers unveiling their carved Lincoln
sitting in his memorial, inviting all to stand
beneath his feet.

From under the weighted layers of loss,
shedding the sheave's confusion,
and fear—slowly, like granite,

the Italians surfaced into America.

VI.

Police chief Hennessy. They loved him in New Orleans,
the way he had caught criminals

with his own hands and towed them
down to the station.

Waterfront gang violence—
the Matrangas and the Provenzanos,

he wanted none of it.

He wanted people to be able to sit on their porches
and read the paper in peace.

He might have named names,
pointed fingers at a trial.

But someone shot him dead.
His dying words, "Dagoes did it."

Suspects were brought to court,
and all found innocent.

But people weren't satisfied.
"Bribery!" they claimed, though the jury

defended the verdict.
"Kill the Dagoes," the crowd cried

as they broke through the prison doors,
and pulled out eleven men, and shot them.

"Hennessy Avenged" read the headlines.
"We had no choice," they claimed,

but to take the law into our own hands.
None were indicted. Too many had taken part.

VII.

The government's immigrant quotas
staunched the flow from the motherland.

Then, World War I arrived.

Used to sacrifice, what was one more
if through their blood,

they could be born

as citizens of their new world?

Lost legs or lost arms—
if at the end of the trenches they dug,

the mud and the mustard gas they endured,

their families could walk the streets
of New York, San Francisco, or New Orleans

and feel whole,

if they could return
and know they were coming home,

they would do what the old ways
told them men are meant to do.

They would go.

VIII.

In the distance, a gray overcast.
Gusts of fog. Vaporous drifts

string across continents,
thicken, and drape over meadows.

In Italy, they had a leader
who believed in unity.
He built up the army, wanted carte blanche authority,
and the world to give his country respect.

"A good beating did not hurt anyone," he suggested.
He wanted space for his people to grow, vital space

where revolution and tradition held hands,
where his power and land could expand like the Romans.

Thunderously, his voice exploded,
shifted and sank to weighted whisper,
then rose and shook the crowds with lightning.

"Give up your gold for the Fatherland," he cried,
"your earrings, and your wedding rings.
Melt them into bars for the national bank."

The immigrants who had had enough of government stories,
who needed their new country so they could get their families going,
didn't file the papers that made them citizens.

Did Americans know if Mussolini
meant anything to Italian Americans
when the government required
them to register as enemy aliens,
forbade them to travel

more than five miles from home
without permission?

Radios, flashlights, cameras—
these could be dangerous signaling devices
the government said. Italians without American citizenship must give
them up.

Leave your life on the Pacific,
the government told Italian Americans. Move inland
and give us your fishing boats
for the war.

The fog bank rolls in, one giant shoulder
leaning, a damp hand at the end of its long arm

pulling 2,100 Italians into custody, relocating 10,000,
restricting the movement of 600,000.
In California, Oklahoma, Maryland, Louisiana,
Tennessee, Texas, and Montana, 26 states in total,

internment camps waited for enemy aliens.

400 Italians were sent there.

A hidden sun pivots
and drops.

Silently,
dark
descends. The world
bends into itself, curls
into the cold—clouds
cover all
in veiled
white.

IX.

How do you know when you're home?

Do you look up one day
at leaves falling from a tree
in a litter of yellow

as you walk out your door,
turn the corner, and know
something has ended, gone cold,

something else been made new?

You walk in this world
and somehow you belong,

though it never is quite home.

But neither is the place
you came from now.

You run through
the silvered names of family
you loved and left,
the hills you walked,
the stones you climbed, the sea.

But none of them is really dead.
The lost papers and loves, worn shoes
and calloused hands, the smell of sausages sizzling in the pan—
all the histories and memories that have brought you
to where you now stand,
tell you you are of two worlds.

You will never belong.

To make a family, to do good work.
Just to live this day, this life—

to break the daily bread,
to drink this cup

to laugh sometimes, and sing
with your children

that is enough, you say.

That is all.

IV. Starting Again

THE DREAM

I lost myself when they took them from me—each child but Arduino
to St. Vincent's orphanage, and I, left alone, without English, without
skill. Beaten. That is how Arduino found my Gaetano that wet

December night—discarded like cut hair or loose threads. Thieves—
they carried off his years of hard work—our dream. They tore away
our children's future with their rough hands, left us clinging

to threads. Beaten, and thrown on the street, covering
the truth in the pretense of reports. But this is clear,
the police did not name or chase the criminals.

Dazed, mute, and without English or citizenship papers,
my sky filled with December clouds shouting with thunder.
An immigrant beaten by fate, what could I do?

I had no power, nothing to offer. Beaten like a rug, my children
fell from me. The state swept them away like so much dust.
I had no education. January to December, I worked at home

washing sheets, cutting pasta. I am no child to life's stubborn stains,
the yolk of need, the bread I must do without. Like Mr. Ghirardelli,
Gaetano and I came to America on a thread. But we had no chocolate

carried in from a foreign world like him to stir into our lives
to sweeten or save us. We had children, all hungry,
needing clothes, a sound bed. Without them, what is life?

What does a dream look like when you lie alone,
carried away into infinite emptiness, your spirit drifting off
into fog—each child floating out into a foreign world?

Gaetano gave his last haircut that December evening,
then closed the door forever. Every day now is December.
I want to be stronger than Calabria's stony streets,

stronger than the threads I wove when I still lived there.
Isn't love stronger than death?
Beaten. Broken. Forsaken. Christ was all that and more.

But I am no Christ. I feel a child myself now, drifting, floating.
A storm has come. The river has flooded and carried my children,
my husband, my spirit away in a rush of mud. Without family, I'm

a stone, tossed down, rolled over by water. Without my dear ones' feet
scuffling through the house, their faces at the table, what is life?
December stretched its bony fingers into my life's soft pockets

and carried my happiness off into the darkness. Oh mother, father,
lost in the skeins of the world I left long ago, I see you now
standing in the yellow heat beaten down by sun and cloudless skies,

by the hard, hard land. Here I am, your broken child, left alone
shuddering at the void—as I left you without understanding
dreams' drums can fall silent. December blows across the sea.

I reach for your love's threads.

OLD VERSUS NEW, GIOVANNI'S EDUCATION
The Second Son's Story

I've always walked between my parents' world,
and the world outside. Papa believed in the *via vecchia*,
the old way. For him, good education meant respecting
traditions. He complained about the lines

he had to step between. For him, life was a ball of knotted string,
not like the world Mama knitted together for him where the yarn
unrolled from a neatly wound form. Papa didn't trust
the powerful—and the powerful took my father from me,

left me with a snarl of yarn wadded up so wrong
I don't know if it'll ever be sorted out.
What was he doing in that Irish club the night he died?
Italians must be careful if crossing neighborhood lines.

Was it an argument about a rise in rent, a move, Papa's defense
of the old ways—some issue of *rispetto*, respect for the family,
when they tossed him on the street? He kept his business to himself—
the *via vecchia*. It was a father's way. He died, and we'll never

know the truth. I'm living at St. Vincent's orphanage now. None of us
live at home with Mama, except Arduino. An eighth grade education,
fourteen years old, and I'm done. Off to work I crawl each morning
into the fog. Old ways, new ways. It's a jumbled knot.

I can't unravel much, but I know this: we'll find a way
to take care of Mama. That's the first thing.
Then, we get the family back together.
Ben educati Papa called it. The heart always counts for more.

AT THE DEL MONTE CANNERY
Luisa at Work

Wheels roll. Machines rattle. The whirl of fruit
spills out onto the belt. Searching, separating,
I sort through each round raw weight that grew
in a faraway sunny field, as if the tumbled fruit could speak.

Spilled out onto the belt, amidst the machinery's roar, searching,
separating, my silent hands reach and retreat, remembering
as if the fruit could speak, the distant orchard the harvest traveled from.
Brought through the water, shaken, skin peeled, and cut;

my hands reach and retreat. Remember, "Keep standing," I cry out
to myself inside the machinery's cacophonous clatter: the day is rising.
A peach, brought through the water, shaken, skin peeled, and cut,
Go on, widow. Fill the tin. Let the juice spill over. Paste the label.

THE WAY ARDUINO REMEMBERS IT

I remember wailing.
The earthquake of her emotion
as she moved from room to room.

The way her body shook—
some rumbling, wild force rose
from deep inside, and broke loose

the night papa died. Her grief fell
from her in enormous sheaves
and crumbled about us.

She wailed, long, great shudders.
We froze, waiting for the next
eruption. But then the sobs ceased.

Instead, she walked out into the garden,
and stood there in the morning light,
the sun coming down on her dark hair

while we stared at her through the window,
tears streaming down her face, and watched
as she ripped flowers from their stems,

furiously yanked weeds from their place,
and flung them away.
When we were little, Papa tossed us

into the air. He sang. He chased us
through the house, shuffling his feet like a train
while we scrambled away laughing.

Mama was the one who sat us at the table
to eat, who sent us to bed each night.
She was the morning sun, the earth

that held us. But without Papa, the engine
was broken. There was no way to mend
the world. She just continued on.

We've talked it over, now that we're older.
Now that all the brothers are back home.
San Francisco had a thousand places to drink

during prohibition. Like all the neighborhood men,
Papa visited the *taverna* in the evening.
But Papa didn't drink much.

The people at the saloon wanted more
than the money in Papa's pockets that December night.
Kicked ribs, contusions on the side of his head,

being thrown from the Shamrock Saloon
into the street to die—that's more
than tossing a man from a bar for being a nuisance.

Though the reports named no one, we brothers
have seen the system at work. Crime doesn't have to be
subtle when those in power want you silent.

Prohibition is creating new criminals. There's a reason
the newspaper mentioned the coroner was checking
Papa's stomach contents. The appearance of searching

for truth is more important than discovering it
when there's something to hide.
Officials didn't follow through on finding

anything. Who are we to pursue an answer
when it could only lead to further harm?

Papa liked to remind us, "We left Italy.
We're in America now.
We've got to act like Americans.

Take care of ourselves," as if
there was the old world and the old ways,
and then there is the new.

But it isn't true.
We're some place in between.
When she came back in from the garden

the day Papa died, we stood at the sink
watching as she washed her hands,
then picked up the cast iron pot

and cut vegetables for soup.
Later, neighbors came by.
They shook their heads. They raged.

How would we go on without Papa,
we couldn't comprehend. But we knew
if she still could cook, we were not lost.

THE SKIN YOU'RE BORN INTO
Luisa Contemplates

I know things men with money don't.
They don't know what it's like to be a woman
who waited ten years without her husband
while he earned the money so she could join him.
So many dreams Tano and I had. Gone now.
They don't know what it's like to lose
the one your children rely on when no one else
can afford to help.

When they killed my husband, they killed me too.
How was it necessary to steal money and life
from a simple barber? He was my children's father.
How could he be worth so little
that those who harmed him gave no mind
to their actions, held no concern for their effect
on this middle-aged woman with sagging breasts
and low shoes, that they thoughtlessly destroy
her and her family? Does having money, speaking English,
going to the right church make a person
worthy to be called a citizen? They count themselves
powerful businessmen, leaders, but could learn a lot
from a woman who knows how to serve.

I'm held with little regard but can't change my face,
my history. I may not speak English or be able to read the forms
for citizenship, but I can read kindness in hand or face,
can translate a subtle knife behind words.

I'm a woman with a small life, but I know
who I am. Like smoke winding its way
through air, I can make myself felt.
My love for my children is more powerful
than greed.

My father left my mother, but the family
remained. My first son died. Gaetano left me in Italy
when he went to America. I work my way through obstacles
like water. I know my task.

Today, I do laundry, hang clothes on the line,
empty cotton arms and legs flapping in dry air—
ghosts of who we are, and all the space in between.
These are the pieces of fabric we wear
into the lives we are becoming.

Somehow, we're always incomplete.
What we are is a mystery, even to ourselves.
These coats and clothes are us,
yet not us. We're more than the cloth
we wrap ourselves in. Daily we put on
these shirts and dresses, fill the emptiness
inside the sleeves and lives we walk around in.
But there's always a hunger, the questions
of what it means to belong.

Though I want only to wake each day and share
what I have with my children, to live
each year aware of the sun coming down, see
the ocean stretching before me in open arms—
the law stole my life when the state took my children from me.

I need to give my children the blessing of their own beds,
to serve the foods I know nourishes them,
teach them stories to live by—dreams.

This is the skin I was born into, what it means
to be a citizen in the world I know, how I live
into the future one day at a time: I give
what I want to be given. This is the greatness
I seek from this city's bosses and leaders, humility
enough to see need, some semblance of compassion.

CHIARA'S STORY

Oh the names, the names of everything lost
that mama lost, yes—her father, to who knows
what foreign world he set out for, and perhaps found
or didn't—no word was ever heard, except that he'd died.

Her husband she lost to the hands of the men
who rolled him for his money, and took his life.
Then the government sent her boys to orphan homes,
though eventually she got them back.

Yes, she lost that house and the life she woke up into
each morning, the boys running through the rooms,
wrestling and restless, calling her name for this or that,
but I lost too. I lost not just my mother, but my home in the world.

She left her mother when she sailed across the sea
for America, but she left me when Papa died.
She fought for the boys, to bring them back
from their orphan homes, but she did not fight for me.

Maybe she thought I was strong enough without her—
that I knew how to get what I needed
in that other house with the blond-haired family.
Somehow, I must have fooled my mother

when I chased my brothers around the front room,
my loud voice demanding what was mine—
the toy they took or the food.
Maybe she thought I had to learn like she did,

how to get used to foreign places,
to rooms without faces, how to forget
the words and names you know, get used to the cold,
to losing what you most loved.

For me, that was her.

LUISA'S CHOICE

Arduino, my oldest, the state let stay with me.
My other boys were gone a year, living at St. Vincent's,
an orphanage of stone and brick with long hallways
where the sisters gave them food and a bed,
a schedule—not a home,
though I could come visit.

This could never happen where I come from—
children sent to a charity house, an institution,
strangers stuffed away together in stiff, narrow hallways.
Italians take care of their own.
A mother belongs with her children,
but I had no way to provide for them.
I didn't have a say.

I had Arduino, but I needed them all—
Giovanni, Gregorio, Chiara, Goffredo—
needed them with me—their noise and stories,
illnesses and laughter—whatever it might be,
it should be ours together.

The boys had each other,
but I couldn't send Chiara to the orphanage.
A charity house was no place for her.
Though she protested, I would spare her that at least.
The state sent her to a home
and encouraged me to get work.

"You can get a job at the cannery,"
Tano's cousin, Amadeo and his wife, Delfina encouraged.
"You don't have to speak English.
The workers are Italians. Women. Friends."

Women worked at home. This was the way I knew—
how life was in Calabria, not how it would be
if Gaetano were here.

But I wanted my children, and this wasn't
Italy. Gaetano was gone.

We were in America.

Peeling peaches, slicing tomatoes.
I could do that.
I chose this path with Gaetano.
This is what we exchanged our world for.

I am following it without him now.

It is my path,
the children's and mine.

LUISA'S GARDEN

I was a weaver. If things went wrong,
I unraveled the cloth.

I'm no longer a weaver, but here I am,
unraveling again.

I stand at the conveyor belt and hold out
my hand for fruit, same as I stood with the distaff

and spindle, pulling on wads of wool, turning them
into thread. Now it's cans waiting to be filled, stretching

continuously along the cannery's spinning belt,
never with the fresh fruit from the yard.

Never from food growing on the windowsill.
It's a big system now—a machine. A factory.

Like empty lives waiting to be filled, the tins
move by. Each one carried along

like prayers day after day—the same lives,
same prayers—for the children, for food.

Life is bigger, though, than what I do or feel.
I just keep on, as one after the other the cans

plod past. Like those who came to Cosenza's shrine
in Paola near where I was born, we're all pilgrims

traveling down the road, longing for something
that can never quite be named.

When I get home, I go to my garden to weed a little
and feed the ducks, see if the goose has laid an egg.

Some people need mountains to climb to prove
their strength. I don't have anything to prove.

I've climbed my mountain. I'm here. I'm alive.
A few flowers, though, color glowing through the heat

or fog, a few bees humming as they work—
that makes me sing.

GOFFREDO'S MUSIC

I didn't want to carry a gun. I loved music, singing, dancing—
the whirl of a radio melody, but there I stood with my brothers

on Mama's steps shuffling our feet the last night before leaving
for the war. Mr. Battistessa, twenty years a locksmith here,

and they forced him to give up his business, lose his home.
A sixty-five year old man was suddenly a threat—

had to be relocated. Mr. Hoover didn't need a reason
to detain you. No crime, evidence or charge required,

only a name like Protto, Sabatini, Giouliotti, or DiMaggio.
Executive Order 9066. That was the explanation.

No exceptions allowed. When not a citizen, what hope
would my mamma have had for not being taken

to an internment facility in Missoula or Crystal City?
We couldn't risk losing her. So, partly from fear, partly from love,

my brothers Giovanni, Gregorio and I joined the army.
No moon lit our way the night we left her house.

"You come home," she said. "I'll be here waiting."
No words to hold the fear blanketing us, we circled Mama,

arms woven around each other. We weren't certain
what trembling we'd face in days ahead.

Straggling down the steps, we scuffled across the street
into the chill air. Mama stood frozen to the landing,

hand against her heart. That was a world
to come home to.

And we did. All three of us brothers.
Like music, falling through an adagio of final notes,

we returned—perhaps not whole, but home.
Sundays, family would come to Mama's to eat and visit.

Opinions rattling the room, I'd leave the relatives to argue
and consult, and call the children to come listen

to Ben Selvin's band play "Blue Skies." Sheets fluttering
in the crisp California sun, the children flung themselves,

whirling and tumbling, across the backyard grass, music
enveloping us with wide arms from an open door or window.

Later, resting on the lawn, we'd stare up into the sky, naming
the August clouds' shifting shapes rolling by while

Hoagy Carmichael's effervescent "Stardust" piano sprinkled
through our ears or Caruso's "Una Furtiva Lagrima,"

burrowed into our bones. Leaping and twirling into the radio's
rising riffs and rhythms or lying on the earth absorbing melodies

with drifting clouds, we weren't Italian Americans
or American Italians. We sang, and we had no thoughts

of whether we weren't enough or too much of anything.
We danced, we dreamed, and no matter how lonely, strange

or hard the world seemed, music wrapped even the sad stories
in harmony. World War Two was over.

A baseball flying above the world, music caught
and tossed us into its sweet glove center—stung us with life.

LUISA FINDING A WAY

Lights shine on San Jose Avenue—a yellow warmth curling back
the twilight edges, mists clearing into stars above, though I can't

yet see them. They've built the bridge across the bay now,
traffic flowing forth and back between the peninsula that before

was cut off. Giant red towers reach across the water, 80,000 miles
of cable holding it together. When he was alive, Tano was my bridge

from the world of Calabria to this one here in California.
Though he was stubborn and temperamental, his middle name

was Pacifico, peaceful. He called me his light. He held me,
the children, held us all with his iron red heart. He loved us.

The boys, Chiara, they're all grown now, live nearby.
Every day, they go to work here in America. They read.

They write, speak English—it's more than I can do.
Always lived in Italian neighborhoods, what was the need?

Still, forty years in America, you'd think I'd speak English.
Maybe I should've learned, but I'd already lost my father,

my first child, my country, my husband. To let go
my language, too, to thoughts choked in foreign sound—

I couldn't do it. Gilbert Street, and Shotwell, Capp, Howard Street
to San Jose Avenue—I've moved houses so many times now.

I've got my own job, make my own rules, live a life women
never would've had where I grew up. The boys have all chipped in

to help make me feel at home. But I'm not Italian, not American.
I can't go back to anywhere I came from. No cable can connect

the worlds I've lost. When I was young, I saw storms move in
across the sea. Clouds like great, dark mountains, bore down

on the shore, battering the coast in a windy torrent.
Here in San Francisco there's plenty of fog, but then

there are days like today, too, New Year's.
Mariano and Chiara walk over from Dolores Street.

Giovanni brings the kids up from San Carlos. Gregorio
and Goffredo are already here, and I make them all

sit down for dinner. I bring out minestrone, pasta
and meatballs. Everything I can. When they've finished,

the children run into the backyard with the ducks to play.
Loss—moving—waiting—and an endless routine

at the cannery. My life has been all of these.
But then, there are days like today

when the sky's so clear, every leaf edge
and building corner is cut sharp as diamond.

RECLUSE—GREGORIO EXPLAINS

Giovanni told his stories after the war,
if you'd listen, the Battle of the Bulge, bombs blasting
while he ran through fog and mud, a German
that shot a bullet through the top of his helmet
but missed his head. 181,000 men dead.
Giovanni's stories were his survival.

Not mine.
Along with 500,000 others of Italian descent
the three of us brothers joined the army,
leaving Arduino to help at home.
We didn't join for adventure or to save the world.
We joined to protect Mama.
With papa dead, she was all we had.
No government man—no one could question
the family's loyalty, send her
to an internment camp if three of us
joined the army—though even that
wouldn't have been true. Safety doesn't come
from locking up or walling out.

They called it the "good war," but I wonder,
What did sacrifice bring? Do I feel more complete,
more American? After the first World War, Wilson
planned to "make the world safe for democracy."
But what is democracy when not everyone's safe—
when Italians, Japanese, and Germans who did nothing
but grow vegetables or sell shoes are put in internment camps
in freedom's name? Freedom is select—
for those already free—who don't have to be careful
about the street they walk down, how they might look,
the accent in their voice, the histories they might bear.
I don't trust authority controlled by money and fear
that uses me to build its own power—
reinforcing and protecting the world it owns.

We won the war, but nightmares haunt me.

Winter's mist rose from the Ardennes like white ghosts
the morning of the battle, as if we were watching
the earth release our spirits before we'd passed on.
Suddenly, searchlights exploded the gauzy veil, detonating
the frozen darkness. What could my brother Ardy know
about long hours waiting behind narrow tree trunks,
hunkering down into icy holes or seeing someone's head
blown off, wondering when your life would end?
Sleeping in San Francisco on clean sheets
every night, Ardy went right on having a good time.

And what is a good time? I don't know.
Don't feel like going out.
Don't care about travel either.
No need to return to the old country
to find what happened to grandparents or where cousins live.
My parents loved their homes but left.
Too much pain to reach now for any old identity.
Too much grief.
Shattered forests riddled with eroding trenches,
decaying boots and broken bodies, homes
blasted from their foundations—
I saw as much of Europe or anywhere
as I ever want to see.

I went to dinner at Mama's every Sunday
after the war, sank with relief into her kitchen chair,
spooned down her soup, *stracciatella* to settle the stomach
or *zucca* with thyme—salvation can be simple.

My bones had turned cold.
I'd killed men— watched their mouths go limp,
legs crumple, their faces press down into the snow.

I'm not interested in heroes.

The dinners kept me going 'til she died.
We went to war for her so the family could eat together.
Papa taught us to keep the old ways,
and we did. Now she's gone.

I'm hungry for a world that'll never be mine.
No meal makes up for what I've seen.

Like a melody learned as a child
that you never forget, Mama meant for me to hold on
to the stone she gave me from home to carry to battle.
But between splintered bodies and broken earth,
without knowing the moment it fell into the dirt's
dark pocket and crushing silence, I lost it—
as if it were refuse, buried beneath a hill
I can no longer climb, never to be found again.

Had a girl who loved me before the war.
Lost her, too. No, I won't ever marry.
Touching, speaking is too delicate an act
for a man who threw grenades.

American or Italian, it doesn't matter.
All I know is where I am right now,
what is in front of me where I walk.
I keep my eyes open.

Before the war, Italians were at the bottom.
Now, somehow, we pass as white.
In Chinatown they speak of non-Chinese as "ghosts."
I'll always be a ghost in someone's world.

Italians keep their secrets,
and I don't choose to pass on the grief.

There are some stories you can't tell
if you want to make other stories come true.
Trouble is, I couldn't get the pictures
out of my head enough to think
of any other story—didn't want anyone
else to live the one I had.

AN END TO IT
Giovanni's Wish

I.

When the kids were growing up and we'd had a good dinner,
I'd tell them to drink water to float their stomachs
so they could eat more. Some things, though,
you never want more of.

The morning Dad died, I stood at the door of that dismal house
on Gilbert Street, staring out into the gray buildings and grime.
The cloth beside him on the bed with the blood he'd coughed up
from being beaten.

I looked at Mama, her eyes fluttering from object to object,
as if a giant black bird had swooped down and carried
our lives away with his. A terrible noise of feet
shuffling through a door. Some giant wave breaking against a shore—
men came and took his body out.

His death: a rock of questions we had for those
who killed him. Government, the *padroni*, and the world,
rolling over us like one of those giant graders
cutting into the earth, and stamping it down
to make a new highway.
Evil exists.

I never wanted someone I loved to be broken like that again.

II.

When we met, Liza and I hiked the hills outside the city. Back then,
it didn't matter that I didn't have a high school diploma

or that at twelve I'd lived in an orphanage
when my dad was killed.

I knew how to work, could make her laugh.
She could sing arias. We were a pair.

III.

During the war, the government
sent Italian and German Americans without naturalization papers
off to internment camps.

I was Italian. Her name was Kruse.

Both our names looked suspect.

IV.

Mama had no citizenship papers, didn't speak English.
She could be sent to a camp.

We knew what it meant to be sent away.
My brothers—none of us could allow it.

If we needed to prove our loyalty, we'd fight.
It was what men did for their families. Liza didn't say no.

V.

Dirt flying, cracked skin, boots without bodies, broken bones,
friends falling with the snow, their faces white as moon, eyes

staring up from the holes inside the earth—

the eyes of birds peering from a nest before
they'd learned to fly.

Splintered light from exploding bombs—
if I had been a bit taller, I'd have been dead.

Before the world turned to smoke,
I believed there could be a need for war.

Not now.

I remember the barrage of artillery fire
as we hid behind trees, crawling through snowdrifts,
the explosions and black dirt
falling on white drifts. The cold.

My brothers and I fought for America to protect mama,
but we hated the cold, the shattered trees,
the splintered limbs, the killing.
The war had blasted a hole into the family.
Italian or American—what mattered?
How did we go on living when so many others died?
Over and over, I told the stories to try and understand.

VI.

I took the children down to Pescadero
for a day at the beach. They played while wave after wave
clattered against the shore.

Something excruciating in the crush of water,
the seagull's cry, a wildness in the waves,
the way the sun
splintered into white glints.

The silence hidden beneath all the noise.
A smooth pebble between the rocks—I had to test God.

I climbed out to the cliff edge where the children
couldn't hear, and shouted at Him above the surf,

called the waves to crash over me, tumble me.
The water's fist. The chips of sky. The ragged, white roar.
Rock. I didn't wash away, though.

Instead, I floated up, as if He were the water,
lifting me, telling me to go on.

And I did.

   VII.

Tradition, language—you can't hold on to these
like Momma did, wearing black every day of the year
after Papa died. Americans thrive on what's new, on change.

"Teach me Italian," my son Pietro said, wanting to know,
but I speak a *calabrese* dialect. It's not the same.
Besides, we're American, not Italian. Why would I teach him

what others called the enemy aliens' language
when it would only bring him questions and fear?

   VIII.

I got my high school education eventually,
took courses for equivalency. Drove a grocery truck

for thirty one years, then retired. Mama's been dead
decades now, and the kids are grown—

Joseph drives a truck, Pietro's teaching art in Singapore.
Why he didn't stay in America I don't know.

Daniella's got the boys. I bring Julia and Melia groceries
when I come by: corn, peas, pork and beans—

good stuff, all on sale, give the grandchildren cookies
to wear as rings, make them eat their cereal. Hot or cold,

they sit there till it's done. If I'd done things the things
they do when I was their age, my teeth would've been

smiling from across the room. Most of the children
have gone to college, though. "Be independent!"

I taught them, and they've found a way into the world.
I save coupons now—have piles on my desk,

but they don't count for much.
I drove that vegetable truck route

ten thousand times or more when I was working.
Probably could've circled the world—all that navigating

so the children could sail across their oceans.
I want them to be well. I give them all I can,

but there's no great dream they have to reach,
no specific occupation or number to attain.

They have to create their own story.
They're moving on, but I am here.

We're family. Presence matters more.
Sometimes, a hand in the dark can be enough.

IX.

I push back the window's curtain.
The stars turn in their bed. Though no one else
sees them, when I look out the window, I can see Jesus

and the three kings in the trees' branches, each one
traveling out, bringing their gift.
Driving the grocery truck all those years,

I thought about how hungry people are.
Moving down the highways, I circled and circled,
always delivering, but the hunger never stopped.

I kept going, kept waking in the morning,
traveling out with the stars, like those wise men did—looking.
Tired. Don't know why I kept going, but I was looking for a sign.

I'm always looking for a sign, just like I'm always
looking for those lost children on the milk carton.
I was looking when I saw the Virgin Mary lying there—

reflected in a whiskey bottle amidst the weeds
in the abandoned lot on the other side of the street.
"Got to come see!" I told the neighbors,

and they lined up to look at her shining from inside
the golden liquid on my mantle. All those years
she'd waited among the weeds,

starlight coming down, the sun, her arms open,
reaching out. Even she doesn't know
when there will be an end to it.

V. Another Generation

JULIA'S FRAGMENTS
A Granddaughter's Quest

Maybe Italian Americans today hold only a few fragments
from their ancestors—the flood of immigrants
that crossed oceans and continents
to exchange their worlds' fabric for a new one
filled with struggle and strangeness:
some addresses scrounged up,
a photo or two, small remembrances
like the flavor of their nonna's meatballs,
but not much on the whole.

Maybe today the world has wrapped itself
into one big ball of thread, and it doesn't matter much
where you came from, whether your grandparents
ate pasta, corn or bread.

But for me, the fragments matter—

street names and occupations, a glimpse
at your ancestor's houses, faces, the single photo that remains.
A food described I'll never taste,
the people and lost worlds, the stories and dreams
my ancestors reached for, the mysteries of their lives
that I can almost see, but not quite—these are the details
and hidden bones that built my life and hold me,
allow me to stand and move through the world.

A pilgrim, I'm searching for the garden of my own origins,
relearning what was pushed aside.
I'm not what the grandparents were.
I can't live inside their culture to understand
their mind or world. Much has been lost
from their way of knowing,
but the emigrants' stories are everyone's pain,

everyone's loss who has ever left home.
The immigrant's loneliness is the world's.

I'll never get their story completely straight.
There'll always be questions.

Maybe my grandparents had difficulty
understanding their own stories,

but the differences of their lives' details
from mine, are treasures
and the journey to discover them important.

To cook traditional foods, listen to music the grandparents
knew or loved, to study their language and history
is to stand under a waterfall surrounded by a river
spilling into an ocean of life. I touch the earth

where my grandparents once lived, and know
I'm part of humanity's enormous trajectory.

PETER LEARNING
A Grandson's Story

My nonna was short, wrapped her hair in a bun and wore
black lace-up shoes. I never met my nonno, though.

He was killed before I was born. For years the family knew little
of who they were—what they loved or longed for in the world

they left or this one. No letters or diary remains—just two photos.
I never heard my nonna speak a word in English,

except when she swore. I couldn't ask her questions, was only nine
when she passed on. In North Beach, I find the address

where Nonno first opened his barbershop in a basement.
Staring down into the blue shadows, I imagine a sidewalk sign

announcing haircuts, picture my nonno hidden behind the doors,
strand by strand cutting out the shape of his life in America.

On Telegraph Hill, I envision him climbing the steps
to his second shop, an open door, scraps of hair scattered about.

It has taken years to piece together a few facts. Did he not
become an American citizen because he wanted to return to Italy

or was the paperwork too much a mystery or a bother—the less
interaction with the government, the better? Whatever the reason,

because of what he didn't do, I can return to Italy, a citizen
if I choose. I picture myself working there on a plot of land

with olive trees and a vineyard, gathering grapes into baskets
while the sun goes down—standing inside the canvas

my sister painted of Italy years ago. Though a citizen,
I'd be a foreigner. It'd be slow work, and hard. Lonely.

I'd need to learn the language and the land.
Something in me would be coming home

to the person I've always been, though couldn't name.
But when I open my front door to the medicinal air

of bay laurel after rain, to the arms of oaks and redwoods
here on the coast south of San Francisco, and step onto

the hillside waiting to be planted with tomatoes, garlic,
basil, and another avocado tree, the earth itself tells me

California is my home. My grandparents braved
much to make this world their home. I doubt I'll ever leave.

House, oaks, bees, sage, sea. The sun lifts its sword,
cuts day from dark. Birds spill through broken clouds.

In this world there is goodness.
I've opened my eyes and have found it.

FAMILY TREE

1875   Gaetano born. Amantea, Calabria, Italy.
1878   Luisa born. San Lucido, Calabria, Italy.

1897   Gaetano and Luisa marry. Amantea, Italy.

    1898   Cosimo born. Amantea, Italy.
    1911   Gianni born. San Francisco, California, USA.
    1912   Gregorio born. San Francisco, California, USA.
    1913   Chiara born. San Francisco, California, USA.
    1914   Goffredo born. San Francisco, California, USA.
    1923   Gaetano dies. San Francisco, California.

    1941   Gianni marries Liza. San Francisco, California.

        1946   Joseph born.
        1947   Giulia born.
        1948   Melia born.
        1949   Pietro born.
        1952   Daniella born.

1961 Luisa dies. San Francisco, California.

TIMELINE

1875   Gaetano's birth. Amantea, Calabria, Italy.
Later becomes a barber.

1877   Garibaldi unifies Italy.
Cuneo's Bakery opens on Green St. in San Francisco.

1878   Luisa's birth. San Lucido, Calabria, Italy.
Later becomes a *filatrice*, a spinner.

1880 - 1924 approximately 4,000,000 Italians immigrate to the US, half of these arriving between 1900-1910. Italian Americans are the fifth largest ethnic group in America.

1890   Police Chief David Hennessy is killed in New Orleans.

1891   Largest lynching in American history of 11 Italians in New Orleans.

1892   Ferry building opened. Second busiest terminal in the world in 1930s.

1895   Mazza threatens Gaetano in his barbershop. Kills 3 wounds 13.
Molinari's deli opens in San Francisco.

1897   Gaetano and Luisa marry in Amantea, Italy.

1898   Cosimo born. Amantea, Italy.

1899   Gaetano leaves for America.
First automobile in San Francisco.

1900   Spreckels Music Temple opens in San Francisco.

1900 - 1904 Bubonic plague, Chinatown. 119 deaths. First plague, continental US.

1901   Labor strike, San Francisco.
Mano Nera or Black Hand operating in San Francisco.

1902   Eugene Schmitz becomes Mayor of San Francisco.

1904   Amadeo Giannini founds the Bank of Italy.

1905 - 1908 Graft trials in San Francisco for Schmitz and his attorney, Abe Ruef for receiving bribes from business owners.

1906   San Francisco earthquake and great fire. 225,000 homeless. 28,000 buildings destroyed. $400,000,000 loss.
Mt. Vesuvius erupts outside Naples, Italy, killing 100 people, and burying towns. Heavy rains follow, creating severe mudslides of ash and water.

1907   Eugene Schmitz imprisoned.
Black Hand brought to trial.

1908   December 28, Messina Reggio tsunami, fire, and earthquake with 7.1 magnitude. Between 75,000 and 100,000 lost their lives.

1909   Del Monte cannery becomes the largest fruit and vegetable cannery in the world.

1910   Luisa leaves for America.
Dec. 24, Luisa Tetrazinni sings on streets of San Francisco by Lotta's fountain.
Arduino born to Luisa and Gaetano.

1910 - 1941 Pete McDonough leader of organized crime in San Francisco. Accused of bribery, perjury, suborning witnesses, tampering with judges, bootlegging, corrupting officials, and controlling and paying off police. Considered the overlord of San Francisco vice, gambling and prostitution.

1911   Gianni born to Luisa and Gaetano.

1912   Gregorio born to Luisa and Gaetano.
First publicly owned mass transport system opened in San Francisco

1913   Chiara born to Luisa and Gaetano.

1914   Goffredo born to Luisa and Gaetano.
World War I begins.

1915   Pan Pacific International Exhibition in San Francisco.

1918   Gaetano registers for draft in Sept. World War I ends in November. Spanish influenza. 650,000 Americans die, more than died in WWI.

1920 Prohibition begins. Black Hand extortion slows.
Women gain the right to vote.

1921 Anarchists, Nicola Sacco and Bartolomeo Vanzetti are sentenced to die for the death of a paymaster for a shoe company, and his guard.

1922 Mussolini becomes prime minister of Italy.

1923 Gaetano dies.
Gianni, Gregorio, Goffredo, and Chiara are taken from Luisa. The boys live at St. Vincent's Home for Boys in Marin County. Chiara lives with a family.
Luisa begins work at Del Monte cannery.

1924 Gianni, Gregorio, and Goffredo return to live with Luisa and Arduino.

1925 Chiara returns to live with her family.

1926 Bombings at Washington Square Cathedral, North Beach.

1927 Sacco and Vanzetti are electrocuted for murder despite worldwide demonstration in support of their innocence.

1928 Bank of Italy becomes Bank of America.

1929 Great Depression begins.

1933 Prohibition ends.

1937 Golden Gate Bridge opens. The bridge used 80,000 miles of cable wire, and cost $35,000,000.

1939 World War II begins.
End of Great Depression.

1941 Attack on Pearl Harbor.
Gianni marries Liza.

1942 FBI arrests 1,521 Italian aliens. Executive Order 9066, called for the enforced relocation of more than 10,000 Italian Americans, and restricted movements of more than 600,000 Italian Americans throughout the US. 264 people of Italian descent were interned for up to two years in the War Relocation

Authority military camps in Montana, Oklahoma, Tennessee, and Texas. In some cases they were relocated together with Japanese Americans who were also interned. Sources regarding the total number of people of Italian descent interned in the US varies between 264 and 400.

1944   Dec. 16 - Jan. 25, 1945 Battle of Bulge. Last major German offensive campaign on Western Front, WWII. 19,276 Americans killed.

1945   World War II ends.

1946   Joseph born.

1947   Giulia (Julia) born.

1948   Melia born.

1949   Pietro (Peter) born.

1952   Daniella born.

1976   Gerald Ford rescinds Executive Order 9066.

1999 - 2000 House Resolution 2442, passed in US House of Representatives in 1999, by the Senate in 2000, acknowledging violation of Italian Americans' civil rights during World War II. Signed by President Clinton in 2000.

APPENDIX

SOUTHERN ITALY

Amantea – A village on Italy's Tyrrhenian coast located in the province of Calabria, approximately 220 miles south of Naples.

San Lucido – A small Italian village on the Tyrrhenian coast located in Calabria, approximately 14 miles north of Amantea.

LUISA'S STORY

Weaving and spinning – Labor was traditionally divided by gender in Calabrian culture. Spinning and weaving were a woman's occupation. Women in villages spun in the traditional way using a drop spindle. Silk has been spun in Calabria since medieval times, and Calabria was one of the most important silk producing areas in Italy and in Europe.

THE CUT

Camorra – A mafia organization originating in Naples in the region of Campania, Italy in the 1800s. They were one of the largest secret criminal organizations. Their activities included blackmail, smuggling, extortion, and robberies.

Mafia – The mafia organization arose out of a power vacuum in the mid 1800s as a form of people's protection against invaders and those in power who ruled the country. They served as armies of people who carried out their own justice apart from the formally ruling authority. A long series of invaders in Calabria created a suspicion of government authority. As a result, Calabrians didn't seek governmental authorities for help in achieving justice or for looking into misconduct because they didn't trust the government as having the people's best interest in mind. Eventually, the mafia became violent and involved themselves in criminal activity. When Italy became unified and the Kingdom of the Two Sicilies no longer existed, the central government asked the mafia to help them. At this point the mafia expanded its power and criminal activity, and wove into the government structure. Mafia members share a code of conduct, loyalty, and silence about their activities.

LUISA EXPLAINS HOW IT HAPPENED

Laundry – Women traditionally did the family's wash in a public space where water was available, as typically water wasn't available inside the home in the early 1800s and 1900s. Usually, stone sinks were present in an outside square in the town where running water was available.

GAETANO'S DREAM

Folk beliefs – Folk and pre-Christian beliefs are mixed with Catholicism in Calabria. The Madonna is an important mediator between God and humans, and people look to her for help in many matters. There is a strong belief in the evil eye, known as *malocchio*, where a person in a state of envy gives another person a bad look, thus causing bad luck. People believed in the significance of dreams, and that goodness wasn't infinitely available, resulting in the necessity to take from one side in order to give to another side. Previously, because modern medicine wasn't prevalent, people often depended on traditional healing techniques such as poultices, herbs, prayer, and candles for healing.

THE WAY IT WAS

Patron saint St. Francis of Paola – Paola is a city north of San Lucido, in Calabria, Italy. St. Francesco of Paola was a Franciscan monk in the early 1400s, said to be a humble man who lived simply. He didn't eat meat or animal products, and advocated nonviolence. When he was dying, King Louis the XI sent for St. Francis of Paola, asking him to be at his side. St. Francis of Paola is the patron saint of seamen.

Cosenza – The capital city of the province of Cosenza, Calabria is located in a valley surrounded by mountains in the interior of the southern portion of Italy. In ancient times, the area was a center for the Brutti tribe who lived in the region before the arrival of the Romans. Before the Brutti, the Oenotrian tribes inhabited the area. The town of Cosenza has been an important place of learning and culture for Southern Italy since ancient times.

LUISA ALONE

Journey to America from Italy – People left their hometowns on foot, train and boat to get to central ports located in Naples and in Genoa. Most people left southern Italy out of Naples Bay and rode in steerage or third class without privacy. This could present problems for women in particular. People were seen as cargo, and self-loading cargo at that. Ships might hold from 1,000 to 2,000 passengers. Once aboard, women were located in one area, men in another, but there could be hundreds of people in the same area with virtually no air circulation. It was noisy aboard ship, and the smell very unpleasant as people often got sick, and water for cleaning yourself was limited. For this reason, passengers preferred to sit on deck during the day. To eat, people might sit on the floor or use benches or shelves, as chairs or tables weren't necessarily provided. The journey took two to three weeks, sometimes as much as a month. On board there was the possibility of getting disease such as cholera. People tend to migrate when the benefits outweigh the costs of remaining where they are.

LUISA CONSIDERS THE FUTURE

Marriage customs and expectations in Italy – In Calabria marriages took place in the Catholic Church and were often arranged. A woman was expected not to have sexual relations before marriage, and marriage was expected to be for life. As women gained more independence as a result of working outside the home, and as Italian Americans interacted more with other cultures after WWII, women were more likely to marry someone not an Italian American.

1908 earthquake and tsunami in Messina and Reggio – On Dec. 28, 1908, a 7.1 earthquake between the toe of Italy at Reggio di Calabria, and Messina in Sicily struck. The quake lasted one minute and killed between 75,000 and 200,000 people. It is, to date, the most devastating earthquake in Europe. Nearly all doctors and nurses were killed in Messina and Reggio. The quake triggered an undersea landslide creating a tsunami occurring alongside the quake.

LUISA'S WORLD

Men in Italy going abroad to work – Because there were few ways to make a living one could survive on, Calabrian men were often gone for much of the year, traveling to northern Italy, to Sicily, as well as other locations for work, sending back some of their wages to the family. Often farm laborers from a particular village moved together as a group through an area as they looked for work. A female head of family in the south of Italy was quite common because of this migration pattern. As a result, women took on more of the roles that were traditionally men's. Many Italian immigrants originally saw their time in the US as temporary, and periodically returned to Italy. They hoped to eventually return to Italy permanently and with the money they saved while working in the US improve their lives by buying land or building a house in the villages they were born in.

Length of time the father of the family was typically living abroad before sending for his wife or family to join him – Seven years was the average number of years, as it took time to raise adequate money for the boat passage, and then also travel by train if one was traveling to other areas of the US once arriving in New York.

Calabria – Calabria is a province located in Italy's southern portion—the toe of Italy's boot. The southern part of current day Calabria was called Italia, from which the country itself attained its name. The Baltic Sea borders Calabria on the east, and the Tyrrhenian Sea on the west. On the north, the province of Basilicata borders Calabria. Almost half of Calabria's geography is mountainous, and contains forests. Historically, the region had trouble with bandits. Agriculture is important to the area, and it is an area that sees earthquakes as well. The region has been inhabited by the Oenotri Greeks, the Brutti, Romans, Visigoths, Ostrogoths Byzantines, Saracens, Normans, Arabs, Swabians, Angevins, Aragonese, Spanish, Austrians, French, and Bourbons. Currently, people in the region speak both dialects from their areas, and standard Italian. The region's main religion is Roman Catholic.

Sila mountains – A mountainous plateau located in Calabria, and the largest mountain range in Calabria.

Telegraph Hill – A neighborhood in San Francisco where many Italian immigrants lived and worked in the late 1800s, the corner of which contains a portion of North Beach.

GAETANO'S ARRIVAL

Ellis Island, Isle of Tears, *L'Isola delle lacrime* – From 1892 to 1954, 12 million immigrants passed through the halls of Ellis Island in New York, going through inspection before officially entering the United States. Immigrants were asked 29 questions, such as their name, age, race, what work they did, their ability to read and write, the address of a friend or relative, and how much cash they had with them. About 40% of the US population today had immigrant ancestors who arrived at Ellis Island.

Mulberry Street – This street is in lower Manhattan, New York City. In the1880s through the early part of the 1900s, Mulberry Street was filled with tenement houses where many Italians lived when they immigrated to the US. It's here that the journalist and social reformer, Danish American Jacob Riis, in an effort to create social change, brought public attention to the extremely poor living conditions of people in the slums.

Tierra del Fuego – This is an archipelago off of the most southern portion of the South American continent.

Countries Italians in the 1900s immigrated to other than the US – Algeria, Argentina, Australia, Brazil, Canada, Chile, Costa Rica, Cuba, Colombia, Egypt, Ethiopia, Germany, Guatemala, Haiti, Libya, Mexico, New Zealand, Paraguay, Peru, Somalia, South Africa, Switzerland, Tunisia, United Kingdom, Uruguay, and Venezuela. Other than Italy, Brazil has the most people who claim full or partial Italian ancestry. Italian immigrants to Brazil typically worked in the coffee fields as laborers or were farmers. The years of greatest Italian immigration to Brazil was from 1880 to 1900. No papers were necessary for immigration to the

US until the US quota system was put in place. The first green cards were part of the Alien Registration Act of 1940.

THE OTHER ISLE OF TEARS

Sid LeProtti – The son of an African American woman and an Italian laborer, LeProtti was a jazz pioneer black piano player of the "So Different Orchestra," also called the "So Different Jazz Band" on San Francisco's Barbary Coast at Sid Purcell's famous dance hall called the So Different Club as well as the So Different Café. The club was located at 520 Pacific Street, also called Terrific Street at the time. Purcell's was a club open to both blacks and whites at a time when this was considered improper.

Barbary Coast – A vice district in San Francisco at the turn of the last century located at Broadway and Pacific Street and named after the Barbary Coast in Africa. A mix of wealth and poverty, the Barbary Coast was an area of crime, prostitution, thievery, liquor, tobacco, and gambling since the time of the California Gold Rush. Musicians from all over the US came to play on the Barbary Coast. The district was at its peak in 1907-1917.

View of marriage vows – Couples married for life in Calabrian culture. Divorce wasn't culturally or socially acceptable. Couples were expected to be faithful to each other.

GAETANO LEARNS FROM A STRANGER

1906 San Francisco earthquake – On April 18, 1906, an earthquake of one minute and a magnitude of 7.8 struck San Francisco and 3,000 people died. Fires burned three days. 225,000 were left homeless. 28,000 buildings were destroyed. The city experienced $400,000,000 in losses. To rebuild the city, forests were depleted. Safety regulations for construction were not taken into account in the rebuilding process. Prior to the earthquake, San Francisco was the main center of industry in California. After the quake, Los Angeles became the center of trade and population, and industry grew to outweigh San Francisco's. Additionally, many artists and writers moved to Carmel in Monterey County after the earthquake. It's believed that Italians helped put out the fire that followed the earthquake by soaking blankets in the wine they had in their basements and then putting the blankets over their houses.

Presidio – A military fortified area of San Francisco.

GAETANO OBSERVES

Bubonic plague, San Francisco Chinatown 1899 – Two stowaways on board a ship arriving from Hong Kong were found to have the plague bacilli. The plague began in 1900 and continued through 1909 when a bounty was put out for rats carrying the fleas that bit people, and the source of transmitting the disease was eliminated.

Golden Gate Park – This 1,017 acre park in San Francisco was approximately three miles long and a half-mile wide. In 1871 under field engineer and commissioner of the park William Hall, and his apprenticed assistant John McLaren's plan, the park was placed in an area that was originally dunes and sand. Streetcars delivered people to the park as early as the 1880s.

Spreckels Music Temple – An oval-shaped open air space, sometimes also called the band shell, constructed in 1900 and located in Golden Gate Park in San Francisco. Industrialist Claus Spreckels, the sugar mogul, donated $75,000 toward the $79,000 construction cost.

City of Rio de Janiero steamer – The City of Rio de Janeiro was a steam powered passenger ship that sailed between San Francisco and Asian ports. On February 22, 1901, while attempting to enter the bay, the steamer ran against a submerged reef. Of its 220 passengers, 135 died.

Mayor Schmitz – Schmitz was mayor of San Francisco from 1902-1907. He was convicted of extortion but the conviction was overturned on a technicality. Schmitz ran again for the office of supervisor in 1921 and won. Schmitz was seen as Abe Ruef's puppet.

Abe Ruef – Ruef was a brilliant though corrupt San Francisco "boss" during a period of corrupt and powerful city bosses. Of the many other government officials participating in acts of bribery and corruption, only Reuf went to jail. He served less than five years and died bankrupt. The big bosses of business and corrupt utilities never went to prison.

1901 labor strike – This was a strike in San Francisco of teamsters (truck drivers) and waterfront workers. San Francisco Mayor Phelan, with the goal of eliminating unions, ordered the strikers to be beaten.

Italians identifying with their regions – The Italian nation state began in 1861. Because Italy was still fairly new when Italians began to emigrate, immigrants from Italy, as a whole, didn't feel a bond with their national identity. Instead, they associated more with their villages, cities and regional areas. They spoke the languages and dialects from their regions, followed the customs of those regions, and tended to live together in their family, village or regional groups when they arrived in America. This pattern was similar to what Calabrians were used to doing as they traveled for seasonal work when living in their home country. This behavior served as a kind of cultural cushion, providing comfort and familiarity that helped immigrants adjust to their new country, but which also could present challenges.

Molinari – A deli in the Italian North Beach district of San Francisco that was established in 1895. It's one of the United State's oldest delicatessens, and has been at 373 Columbus Avenue since the 1906 earthquake. P.G. Molinari was an Italian American immigrant to San Francisco from the Piedmont area of Italy.

GAETANO'S VIEW OF PROTECTION

Pete McDonough – McDonough was a central leader of San Francisco crime life between 1910-1941. The police protected him while quietly managing his illegal vice trade. Among other things, McDonough, was accused of bribery, perjury, suborning witnesses, tampering with judges, bootlegging, corrupting officials, and controlling and paying off police.

Southern Italian attitude toward the church – Calabrians distrusted the church, a sentiment based on experience with church officials in southern

Italy. Italian Catholics appreciated the visual and physical aspects of the church such as the pageantry of ceremonies held at key moments in life to celebrate birth, marriage, and to mark the passage of death—qualities appealing to people who were largely illiterate at the time.

Southern Italian attitude toward government – Calabrians put little trust in social institutions outside the family as Calabria was for centuries a region occupied by foreign powers and absent landlords who didn't have the people's best interests in mind.

James Rolph, mayor of San Francisco – San Francisco's 30th mayor. Rolph was known for his overindulgence in sensual pleasures, and presenting himself as having the values and support of the common person.

LUISA LEAVES HOME

How people left Calabria – People left their homes in Calabria in a variety of ways: by boat, train, by foot, by donkey, by wagon. Sometimes people had to wait a while at the port, and housing was set up there for this purpose.

BECOMING NEW

Amadeo Giannini – Giannini was the son of an Italian immigrant. He founded the Bank of Italy in 1904 that later became the Bank of America. Giannini believed in common people and the work ethic they demonstrated. He provided loans to those affected by the San Francisco earthquake on April 18,1906. His father was killed when he was a boy.

San Francisco earthquake – See above, p. 124, Gaetano Learns from a Stranger, 1906 San Francisco Earthquake.

GAETANO AT WORK

Oldest child's responsibility– In Italian culture, it was traditionally the oldest child's responsibility to take on the father's responsibilities if the father was absent.

Barber occupation – As it was one of the most common jobs for an Italian immigrant, to be a barber was a competitive business, making it difficult for a barber to raise the price of a haircut because there were so many other places one could get a haircut. Barbers' licensing began in 1897. Barbers were inspected to protect public from diseases such as impetigo & ringworm.

Conditions in Italy provoking mass migration – Southern Italy was isolated geographically because of its many mountains and lack of good roads and transport. Problems such as absentee landlords, illiteracy, and diseases such as malaria already existed before the unification of Italy. After unification, the tax structure was set up to favor the industrial north, and southern Italy carried more of the financial burden.

Conditions aboard the boat on trip to America – Conditions were very crowded with a lack of privacy or opportunity to get fresh air or clean properly, as water was in short supply. Many people got sick, and the air smelled of vomit and sweat.

LUISA DESCRIBES A FAMILY CELEBRATION

Pan Pacific International Exhibition – This was a world fair held in San Francisco held in the Marina district from February 20 to December 4, 1915. The fair was in recognition of the completion of the Panama Canal, and demonstrated San Francisco had recovered from the 1906 earthquake. The buildings took over three years to construct, were meant to be temporary, and were made out of plaster, wood and burlap. Exhibits included representations of the Greek Parthenon, the Hotel de Salm in Paris, California's redwoods, and a model of the Panama Canal. Several countries had pavilions at the fair, including Italy, whose cluster of eight buildings surrounding a piazza represented architectural styles of the fourteenth, fifteenth, and sixteenth centuries. A central attraction was the "Tower of Jewels," a 435 foot high tower covered in 100,000 pieces of cut glass.

MAKING A LIFE

Ethnic groups in San Francisco from 1900 to 1930 – Ethnic groups, such as Italians, brought to America local customs, traditions and dialects from their home countries. Living together in San Francisco with others who originated from the same villages or regions helped immigrants adjust to changes they experienced upon arrival in America. As Italian immigrants improved their economic conditions, they tended to leave the Little Italy they'd created in San Francisco's urban center and to move into the suburbs. At the time of the Italian's mass immigration to the U.S., America was a group of many different nationalities working to establish its own identity, and tensions between ethnic groups as well as between Italians from different regions were present.

Luisa Tetrazzini – Tetrazzini was a celebrity of enormous popularity. She sang opera and had a big personality. When she was 39, she was told she couldn't sing in the US unless it was for Hammerstein. In response she stated, "I said I would sing in the streets of San Francisco, for I knew the streets of San Francisco were free." Wearing a white gown that glittered in the light, a boa, and an enormous hat, she sang, among other songs, "The Last Rose of Summer" at Lotta's Fountain on Christmas Eve to a crowd of 250,000.

LUISA'S CIRCLE

Education and the idea of respect in southern Italian culture – Formal education in Calabria was minimal, and not seen as particularly necessary. Because schools were a government institution and governments had severely oppressed the people, families from this region saw educational institutions as opposing the traditional family values and disrupting family unity. Only a few boys extended their education beyond the first few years. Education in American public school system, while helping children born of Italian immigrants, also created a kind of division between parents and children, as it altered and diluted the influence of family values.

Tradition of searching for wild foods – People in Calabria have long used herbs and wild foods such as oregano, fennel, and mushrooms in their food.

GAETANO'S VIEWS OF PROTECTION

Idea of "protection" – Mafia members demanded money from business people in exchange for "protection" of their business as well as "protection" from personal threats or violence by the mafia.

Ideal for Italians of owning your own business – Having a business of your own was seen as a wiser ambition than getting an education because it was a tangible and concrete mark of success.

Prohibition – Prohibition was an era in US history from 1920 to December 1933 when it was illegal to manufacture, sell, and transport alcohol. This was promoted as a social change in the attempt to curb alcoholism and violence in the family resulting from over drinking, as well as to rid saloons of corrupt political practices. Alcohol consumption reduced by half as a result of prohibition. Organized criminal activity related to bootlegging rose during this same time period, however, though some argue this rise was the result of other causes. Rather than stopping people's drinking habits, alcohol consumption went underground during the prohibition. Politicians, such as Warren Harding, continued to drink his scotch, and owned stock in a brewery, but voted for prohibition.

St. Nicholas Eve – December 6 is the Christian celebration of St. Nicholas, the bringer of gifts. St. Nicholas was a Turkish saint who lived in the coastal town of Myra. He is known as the protecting saint of children.

Shamrock Saloon – Owned by Thomas Cullen, the pub was located at 543 Market St. in San Francisco, next door to the Shamrock Ball and Racket Club. It's thought to be the oldest listed handball court in the US. Using one of the pub's walls as the front wall of the court was a common practice in Ireland, and this was how the Shamrock Saloon was set up as well.

DECEMBER

Italian Americans and governmental institutions – Italians didn't look to outside institutions, such as the police, for help as government officials were generally not to be trusted in the environment Italians originated from.

HISTORY I

Scylla – Scylla is the monster in Greek mythology that lives on one side of the Strait of Messina. Charybdis lives on the other. Charybdis was a whirlpool on the Sicilian side, and Scylla a shoal of rocks on the mainland of Italy.

Brutti – Brutti is the name of a tribe that in ancient times (approximately 500BCE) lived in the region now identified as Calabria.

Byzantines – Byzantium was the Eastern Roman Empire whose capital was Constantinople (known today as Istanbul in present day Turkey.) Byzantines were citizens of the Byzantine Empire.

Saracens – This is a term used by Christians at the time of the crusades to refer to Muslims. Later, the term was used more generally to refer to Arabs.

Normans – Normans were the ethnic group in the region of Normandy— an area in northern France. The Norman empire worked to conquer the Mezzogiorno (Southern Italy) piece by piece over a period of 140 years, from 999CE to 1017CE.

St. Francis of Paola – St. Francis of Paola is the patron saint of the province of Cosenza, Calabria, in Southern Italy. Though not an ordained priest, St. Francis of Paola founded the religious order of the Minims. The etymology for minims is from Latin, meaning the smallest. This name was chosen for the religious order because the order's focus was on humility, and St. Francis of Paola endeavored to be the least in the house of God.

HISTORY II

Oenotrian vine cultivator tribe – The Oenotrian were one of the two tribes to settle in Calabria in ancient times, approximately 1500BCE. The other was Italia, from which Italy takes its name.

Garibaldi and unification of Italy – Before the Risorgimento of 1860-1870, when Garibaldi unified the country, Italy consisted of warring city-states, kingdoms and regions. Italy's unification was the result of political, cultural and social movements, at the end of which The Kingdom of Italy was established, and Rome became the capital. At the time of unification, Northern Italy had a free market economy, Southern Italy an economy with a variety of government protections such as quotas and tariffs on imported goods. Unification was not completely successful. Industrialization in Southern Italy didn't improve as a result of unification, and the region experienced a heavy increase in taxes as well. Politicians didn't clearly see the region's need for land reform. Neither did they respond to organized crime or to the government corruption there. Southern Italy's problems pre-existed Italy's unification, however, and were the result of centuries of isolation and domination by foreign powers. Nevertheless, after unification, the region's difficulties were exacerbated, resulting in Southern Italians' mass migration to other countries rather than continue to face the serious and continued hardships they encountered.

Job's plagues – The Biblical story describes Job as a good man who is well off, and who has a series of terrible things befall him. Yet he bears up under all of them. Job loses his animals, his servants, and all his children. His body becomes covered in sores. Regardless of all these difficulties, Job never curses God. Job tries to understand why so much grief has befallen him, but is never embittered over what he has lost. He understands that all he ever had was gift to begin with, doesn't cling to what he once had, and endures everything with patient steadfastness.

Mt. Vesuvius – A volcano located on the Gulf of Naples, approximately five and a half miles east of Naples. It's this volcano that erupted in CE 79, destroying the Roman city of Pompeii.

HISTORY V

Del Monte cannery – In 1909 the Del Monte cannery was the largest fruit and vegetable canning plant in the world, producing 200,000 hand-soldered cans a day, and employing 2,500 people. Women removed pits and cut each peach in half. Containers were filled through a hole in the lid. Production ceased in 1937, a result of the Great Depression. Many women of Italian ancestry worked there.

Al Capone – One of America's most infamous gangsters, Al Capone was known for his criminal connections to bootlegging, gambling, and prostitution in the 1920s and 1930s.

Genaro Broccolo – Known as "The Al Capone of the West," Genaro Broccolo was a mafia member in San Francisco during the 1920's.

Lanza – The Lanza crime family was connected to the mafia in San Francisco in the 1920's and 1930's in the prohibition era.

Rosa Ponselle – American soprano opera singer, singing often for the Metropolitan Opera, Rosa Ponselle is thought to be one of the greatest opera singers of the century because of her voice range.

Eddie Lang, born Salvatore Massaro – Brilliant jazz guitar soloist and virtuoso of the 1920's and 30's, Eddie Lang was the first to bring his jazz guitar instrumental solos into public awareness.

Guiseppi "Joe" Venuti – Venuti was a jazz violinist star, recording with Eddie Lang through the 1920's and 1930s.

HISTORY VI

Police chief Hennessy – Hennessy was investigating mafia criminal activity in New Orleans between the Matrangas and the Provenzanos with the aim to reduce mafia activity when he was killed in 1890.

Matrangas – This is an American mafia crime family in New Orleans connected to extortion and labor racketeering. They were rivals with the Provenzanos in the 1870-1890s. Several Matrangas were arrested for the murder of police chief David Hennessy, but were not found guilty. This resulted in a mob storming the prison and the largest mass lynching in America.

Provenzanos – The Provenzanos were a rival New Orleans mafia crime family to the Matrangas in the 1870-1890s.

HISTORY VIII

Italians during WWII – Italian Americans fought during WWII alongside other ethnic groups and mainstream Americans. This served to help Americans of Italian ancestry to begin to move outside their regional perspectives, and to identify themselves as Americans. Upon returning to the United States at the end of WWII, the GI Bill helped Italian Americans get a college education, leading to economic improvement, and contributing to their move from urban located Little Italies to suburban America.

Benito Mussolini – Mussolini was Italy's fascist leader from 1922-1941. He convinced people he was the strong man who could solve Italy's problems through "law and order." He got rid of civil liberties as well as his opposition, and by 1925 controlled Italy as a dictator. Mussolini sided with both Franco and Hitler, and hoped to create an "Italian Empire." Mussolini encouraged Italian immigrants to stretch their thinking beyond the Italian regions they came from, and to think of themselves as Italians. He motivated them to feel pride in their accomplishments while remembering the nation they came from. This was a new way of thinking for Italian immigrants, as previous to their arrival in America, immigrants strongly identified with the regions they lived in, and had not thought of themselves as Italians.

Internment camps – Fearing people would be loyal to the countries of their ancestry during World War II, the US government forcefully removed people of Japanese, German, and Italian descent from their homes and families, and brought them to prison-like detention areas set up in various US locations. Additionally, people from these nationalities who were living at the time in Latin America were brought to internment camps in the US. In total, there were 68 centers that either processed or held people of Italian, German, or Japanese descent during WW2. Of these, there were nine Justice Department Detention Centers, and 18 US Army facilities where Italian Americans were frequently sent. 10,000 people of Italian ancestry were forcefully relocated. 600,000 people of Italian ancestry were made to register as an "enemy alien."

AT THE DEL MONTE CANNERY

Del Monte Cannery – See description on pages 132-133 under History V.

THE WAY ARDUINO REMEMBERS IT

Family identity and gender roles – Family was of central importance to Italian American immigrants. Coming from a cultural history where invaders had controlled their country for centuries, Calabrian immigrants, like other Southern Italian immigrants, put little trust in social institutions outside the family. A family's father was typically a respected authoritarian figure who was not to be questioned. The father was expected to both protect and provide for his family in addition to controlling his family's behavior and maintaining the family's reputation. The mother was the family's emotional core, teaching children their moral responsibilities and emotional obligations. She ran all aspects of the house—cooking, cleaning, laundering, and managing the family's budget. The woman needed to be sharp and a keen bargainer. Aging wasn't something women were taught to fear, as elders were respected. One's family was given priority over jobs, promotions, economic advancement, and was placed above all other interests. Children bent their desires to the needs of the family, and were given duties and chores. As they grew older, boys were given more freedom and less supervision, though girls were not. Women and girls worked in chores related to the home, and didn't hold jobs outside the home. In the case of an absent father, the eldest son stayed at home with the mother and carried out the family business in the place of the father. Women spent little time in the company of males other than their family members.

THE SKIN YOU'RE BORN INTO

Italian identity in America – Approximately half of the Italians that came to America returned to Italy. Italians were seen as outsiders because they often had darker skin, were frequently illiterate, and practiced the Roman Catholic tradition differently than Irish Catholics. In some places in America, Italians weren't allowed to worship in the same buildings as Irish Catholics. European Protestants came to America escaping tension in their home countries between Catholics and Protestants. This anti-Catholic sentiment was carried into America where Protestants reacted toward them with distrust and sometimes hostility. While arrested no more frequently than other ethnic groups for crimes, Italians were painted as criminal types because of some notorious, well-publicized mobsters. Additionally, in response to conditions experienced in Italy, some Italian immigrants arriving in America were socialists or anarchists. Anarchists occasionally let off bombs in the city. Additionally, American business owners saw socialists who became involved in the trade union movement as troublemakers, and therefore dangerous as sometimes strikes resulted in violence.

Women are seen as being the heart of the family, the nurturing center that holds together the culture. They had many responsibilities. The family relied on the mother for its emotional, moral, and internal strength.

LUISA'S CHOICE

Women, work, and changing roles – To bring in enough income, daughters of Italian families in America went to work, often earning nearly half of the family's income. Women gained more independence as they worked outside of the house, as they were less under the observation and control of male family members. They left the house without a chaperon, met with other women, gained new understanding and skills, and became more fashion conscious. They spoke with men not their relatives, and in situations not chaperoned. These changes contributed to the rise of women wanting a larger voice in the world at large, along with the right to vote. As roles began to change, women felt the responsibility of needing to provide for the children and the household in addition to meeting financial responsibilities of the family.

LUISA'S GARDEN

Effects of industrialization on Italian American family – Southern Italian immigrants were some of the workers with the poorest pay in America. See also "Women, work, and changing roles" under "Luisa's Choice."

GOFFREDO'S MUSIC

Executive Order 9066 – This was an executive order signed by President Franklin D. Roosevelt in 1942 during World War II, ordering people defined as enemy aliens to be removed from the West Coast and sent to internment camps.

Internment camp WWII – See comments under History VIII.

Crystal City – Crystal City was one of the internment camps during World War II for Japanese, Germans, and Italian ancestry and their families. The camp was surrounded by ten-foot high barbed wire fence and guard towers, but also contained food stores, schools, places of worship, and a hospital. At its opening, the camp was 240 acres with 41 three-room cottages and 118 one-room cottages measuring 12x16 feet. At its height, the camp held 3,374 people.

Some considerations as to why people of Italian descent living in America joined the US military and during WWII – People of Italian ancestry were the largest ethnic group in America to enlist in the US military during WWII. One suggested reason for their strong turnout to fight with the US in the war was their desire to demonstrate their faithfulness to the US. People of Italian ancestry were seen as enemy aliens, and therefore suspect. A desire to prove the opposite is another possible motivating factor for their joining the military. Viewing people of Italian ancestry in America as enemy aliens resulted from Italy's dictator, Mussolini, siding with the Central Powers of Germany, Austria-Hungary, and Turkey during WWII. Many men from America of Italian heritage who enlisted in the military had never been to Italy.

Ben Selvin – Ben Selvin was a big band jazz musician and record producer. He is thought to have made more records than others of his era with 13,000 recordings. Some of his famous titles are "Happy Days Are Here Again," "Yes, We Have No Bananas," and "I'm Forever Blowing Bubbles." He began recording in 1919, and recorded for Columbia in the 20s and 30s, as well as for Muzak, and later for RCA Victor and Majestic Records.

Hoagy Charmichael – Hoagy Charmichael was an American composer, singer, pianist, bandleader, and actor, writing such songs as "Stardust," (1927) and "Georgia on My Mind" (1930).

Enrico Caruso – Caruso was an Italian tenor opera singer performing internationally between 1903 and 1920. He often performed at the Metropolitan Opera in New York City. He first sang on the streets of Naples and in cafes to earn extra money for his family.

LUISA FINDING A WAY

Golden Gate – The Golden Gate Bridge was designed by Leo Moiseiff who also designed the Manhattan Bridge. The Golden Gate Bridge is 1.7 miles long, holds 80,000 miles of cable wire, cost $35,000,000, and the color is called international orange, the color of the original sealant. Building the Gate began in January 1933. Work was completed on May 27, 1937. 50,000 people walked across the bridge opening day.

Italian American immigrants and learning English – Many immigrants of Italian ancestry were illiterate or had little education, making it more difficult to become literate in a second language.

Some considerations as to why some Italian immigrants living in the US didn't become citizens – Half of the people of Italian descent who came to America returned to Italy and didn't intend to stay in the US. Those that did stay in the US may not have gotten citizenship because they weren't literate in Italian, making it harder to complete the citizenship process in English as they didn't speak English. They also may not have seen the benefit of becoming a citizen as they could maintain their culture within the home and function as American in the world outside the home.

Change in Italian American women's roles – Women ruled the home and decisions made there. They generally didn't go outside of the home to work and their social connections were largely within their own family structures. Out of economic necessity, women moved into the work world, their social connections broadened, as did their economic status, and their move away from traditional expectations.

RECLUSE—GREGORIO EXPLAINS

Battle of the Bulge – The final German offensive move in WWII on the Western Front. The battle was fought in the Ardennes, an area the Allied forces didn't think a major attack was possible because the area was geographically challenging. The Battle of the Bulge was the largest battle on the Western Front. The Germans' initial attack broke through the Allied forces' defensive line, pushing so far into where they were located they created what looked like a bulge. The battle is named for this. The battle was fought in snowy conditions causing very poor visibility. The Germans hoped to split the Allied forces in two so they would be unable to supply themselves. It lasted one month and was one of the worst battles in WWII for loss of life. 20,876 Allied forces died and 42,893 were wounded. Germany lost 15,652 men, 41,600 were wounded, 27,582 captured. The losses from this battle were so great that Germany was unable to mount another successful attack.

Woodrow Wilson – In declaring war on Germany in a speech before Congress on April 2, 1917, the 28th US President, Woodrow Wilson, said the US's need to help in the effort to "make the world safe for democracy" was the reason the US should break its neutral status and enter into WWI.

Ardennes – This is a large, hilly and forested area whose geography includes folds, faults, uplifting, winding rivers, rocks, and peat bogs. The area extends through portions of Belgium, Luxembourg, Germany and France. In the high Ardennes, weather can be quite inhospitable. European leaders thought it would be so difficult to maneuver tanks through the area that it was left undefended during WWII.

Sunday dinners – Traditionally, Italian American families came together to eat dinner, usually at the grandparents' house after mass. The dinners involved the extended family where the women cooked and people caught up on the family events.

Chinatown – The area of San Francisco on Grant Avenue and Stockton Street where the Chinese immigrants centered themselves. It is the oldest Chinatown in America.

Italians and Secrets – A family's business traditionally stays private in Italian culture.

World War II's effect on Italian Americans' social status – Upon returning to America after the war, the GI Bill helped Italian Americans get a college education. This contributed to economic improvement for Italian Americans, as well as to their move away from Little Italies in urban areas out to America's suburbs.

AN END TO IT

Italians workers – Because many Italian immigrants were illiterate and without training, they often took menial jobs as laborers and jobs that many other laborers didn't want to do. Women typically worked at home. Italian Americans and their offspring chose and remained in blue collar skilled, semi-skilled, and unskilled jobs longer than other ethnic groups, possibly because they preferred working with their hands, and because for them, work was for the purpose of giving to those you love—your family. Work should not distract from your time with your family.

GLOSSARY

bambini—children. (Gaetano's View of Protection)

ben educati – well behaved, raised well. (Old Versus New, Giovanni's Education)

Camorra – a mafia organization originating in Naples in the region of Campania in the 1800s. They were one of the largest secret criminal organizations. Their activities included blackmail, smuggling, extortion, and robberies. (The Cut)

Camorristi – members of the secret crime organization, the Cammora (Gaetano's Arrival)

cannoli – an Italian dessert consisting of a tube-shaped pastry shell filled with sweetened ricotta cheese, and often containing with pieces of chocolate or nuts. (The Other Isle of Tears)

cholera – a disease spread through contaminated water or food, and caused by a toxic bacterial infection of the stomach leading to dehydration and diarrhea, also causing muscle cramps and vomiting. Though it can cause death, it's a treatable disease. (History II.)

citron – a fragrant citrus fruit that looks similar to a lemon but larger with a much thicker rind, and a typically rougher and bumpier surface. (Gaetano's Arrival)

contadini – peasants, sharecroppers, small landowners. (History I.)

dago – a derogatory word used to refer to Italians. (History V.)

dolci – sweet, dessert. (The Other Isle of Tears)

enemy aliens – a foreigner living inside a country that is at war with the country the citizen originates from. (History VIII.)

guinea – a racial slur and way of saying an Italian is dark skinned like the natives of Guinea and not white. (History V.)

gnocchi – small, light dumplings made with potato and flour, and served with a sauce. (History V.)

granita al caffe – a dessert of icy slush with granular texture made with coffee and sugar. (The Other Isle of Tears)

internment camps – forced relocation and imprisonment of people of Italian, German and Japanese ancestry during WWII into concentration camps located in various interior areas of the western US. (History VIII.)

Isle of Tears, *L'Isola delle Lacrime* – another name for Ellis Island, so called because some people who were hopeful of entering the US were turned away, thus losing the opportunity to achieve their dreams of creating a better life. (Gaetano's Arrival)

limoncello – a liqueur made with the zest (or peel) of lemons and grappa, vodka, or grain alcohol, and mainly produced in Southern Italy. (History V.)

mafia – an organization involved in criminal activity and sharing a code of conduct and loyalty. They are silent about their activities, and other Italian Americans didn't want to point them out, possibly out of fear of repercussions from getting involved. Italians were not the only ethnic group involved in mafia activities during prohibition. The Irish, Jews and Italians formed relationships to carry out their work. (The Cut)

malaria – a mosquito-born illness that giving a person parasites that cause fever, chills, shaking, nausea, headache, fatigue, sweating. Malaria damages red blood cells as well as the kidneys, and can lead to death. (History II.)

Mano Nera – a phrase meaning Black Hand. A method, not an organization, of extorting money from people by sending them letters with threatening people with kidnapping, bodily harm, murder or arson if they didn't handover a specified amount of money at a particular location. The notes were typically accompanied with drawings such as a knife dripping with blood or a skull. It was common for Italian immigrants to America before the time of prohibition to be threatened in this manner. (Gaetano's Views Of Protection)

Mezzogiorno – literally meaning midday, but referring to Southern Italy or the area of Italy formerly known as the Kingdom of Naples. This portion of Italy is very sunny at midday. (Gaetano's Arrival)

nonna – Italian for grandmother. Some people also called their Italian grandmother nonni. (Peter Learning)

nonno – Italian for grandfather. (Peter Learning)

oxheart tomatoes – large tomatoes that can weigh up to three pounds. Pinkish in color, and shaped like a heart, the tomatoes are sweet and juicy. (Gaetano's Arrival)

patron saint – in Roman Catholicism a holy person who has died and is chosen by a person, family, region or country as a special protector who will pray for and guide them. (The Way it Was)

padroni – overseers, elders, bosses, bureaucrats, masters, employers typically who exploit their immigrant workers. (An End To It, I.)

protection money – Italians were often coerced into paying people off with money so that they or their business wouldn't be harmed. (Gaetano's Views Of Protection)

rispetto – respect. (Old Versus New, Giovanni's Education)

saint day *festa* – feast day honoring a local saint. (Luisa Alone)

shanghaied – kidnapping someone using violence or some other devious means to trick a person, commonly by drugging their drink. Typically, the person would wake up aboard a ship needing a crew, and would then be forced to work. (The Other Isle of Tears)

stracciatella – a type of egg drop soup containing scrambled egg in broth with semolina and parmesan cheese. (Recluse—Gregorio Explains)

strano paese – strange country, foreign country, foreign village. (Luisa Alone)

tarantella – a folk dance of southern Italy employing a fast tempo in 6/8 time, and using quick steps involving spinning. The dance is connected to the story that when bitten by a tarantula spider, the way to counteract the poison's effect was to dance with the tarantella's frenzied rhythm. Considered a courtship dance, it was also thought to have the ability to cure illness, as well as the ability to cure a woman who was frustrated or depressed. The tambourine is often used in the dance. (History II.)

taverna – a small restaurant serving drink and food. (December)

tenement – an old apartment house in a city, typically crowded in need of care. (History V.)

testa dura – hardheaded, stubborn. This character trait is a stereotype of Calabrians. (Gaetano's Views Of Protection)

wop – a pejorative term for an Italian, coming from the Neapolitan word *guappo* meaning swagger. (History V.)

via vecchia – old ways, following traditional customs. (Old Versus New, Giovanni's Education)

zucca – a pumpkin. (Recluse—Gregorio Explains)

DISCUSSION QUESTIONS

1. How do the physical and social aspects of the settings both in Calabria and in San Francisco affect characters' choices? What central events or experiences motivated Gaetano to move to America? Is this different than Luisa's motivation?

2. What risks were involved in Gaetano and Luisa's immigration to the US? Were the risks worth the problems they encountered as a result of immigrating?

3. What evidence do the poems give for why Italian immigrants were seen as strange or different? What evidence is in the text for why Italians were seen as outsiders in America? What made Italian Americans seem strange and fearful to others?

4. What are central reasons the narrative gives for why Italians immigrated to America? How are these similar to or different from stories of immigration we read about in the news today? What is similar or different in the kinds of hardships or difficulties they experience?

5. How does the narrative reflect the value of family? How are these values similar to or different from values in your own culture?

6. What values does the family hold as most important? How do their values affect decisions they make when confronting hardship? How does the family's socio-economic conditions affect their choices?

7. What social forces might have influenced the family's choice not to seek a doctor or to seek help when Gaetano was injured?

8. Where is home for the family? What personal and world events occur that make it virtually impossible for the family to return to Italy? In what ways does the story reflect the difficulty of making America home? What does the text infer about what home means for Italian immigrants to America?

9. What clues does the text give regarding Italian American family structure and values?

10. In what ways did Gaetano's death change the family? How did it affect Luisa's sense of herself in the world?

11. What was Executive Order 9066? How did it change the family's life? How did WWI and WWII influence Italian Americans, according to History VII? How did World War II influence people in America of Italian ancestry?

11. How do Luisa's ideas about her gender, social role and her self-identity change over time? What is the effect of these changes? What does she gain as a result of the changes? What is lost? What does society in general gain or lose as a result of these changes in perspective regarding gender?

12. Does Luisa choose her role as nurturer or is it chosen for her?

13. How do Gaetano's choices reflect traditional male roles and values? How do they differ?

14. How do characters demonstrate both fear and generosity in their lives? How do events in characters' lives reflect other characters' attitudes of fear or generosity?

15. In the poem, "The Skin You're Born Into," what is Luisa's central argument? What lines in the poem, "The Skin You're Born Into," reveal the themes of loss, dreams, and the need to belong? How are these connected in this poem, and how does this poem connect to these themes in other poems or in the text as a whole?

16. What parallels do you see between Luisa and Gaetano?

17. How do Gaetano and Luisa's social and economic positions affect their choices in life?

18. What words in the poems reveal who holds what kinds of power?

19. In the poem "Gaetano's View of Protection" Gaetano is cynical about political leaders and leery of people who want to protect him. Why is this? How would you describe Gaetano's attitude toward religion and authority figures? What lines in the text support your analysis? How does Gaetano's view of authority affect his choices as well as his family's?

20. How does money influence choices authority figures make in the narrative?

21. How does Gaetano's occupation of a barber, and Luisa's of a spinner affect the word choices in their narratives?

22. Where are specific places in the text where word choices the author uses are especially effective in creating an emotional response from a reader?

23. How does the title, *A Space Between*, connect to the narrative? In what ways does the family occupy a space between and what is significant about that in-between state? What lines from the text support the interpretation?

24. The poem "Luisa's Circle" refers to lines the family needs to be aware of in the outside community. What is she referring to? What invisible boundaries does the family need to be aware of in America and why?

25. How do the poems reflect tension and differences amongst the Italian Americans in the Italian American community? What reasons are given or implied in the poems for this tension?

26. How does the author's choice of narrative poems in alternating voices influence your understanding of events such as Gaetano's death?

27. How do the different voices telling the story in the text add to and create a larger composite picture of the events in the family's experience

in becoming American? What does the text reveal about different people's interpretation regarding what it means to be American?

28. In the poem, "History V." What is meant by the lines that say, "How much new can a person bear / before the world he knows breaks?" How does this idea appear in other parts of the narrative?

29. In the poem, "History IX" What is meant by the words "You will never belong?" How is this idea revealed in other poems?

30. How do characters differ regarding their views of what it means to be American?

31. In the poem, "The Skin I Was Born Into," Luisa says,

> Today, I do laundry, hang clothes on the line,
> empty cotton arms and legs flapping in dry air—
> ghosts of who we are, and all the space in between.
> These are the pieces of fabric we wear
> into the lives we are becoming.
>
> Somehow, we're always incomplete.
> What we are is a mystery, even to ourselves.
> These coats and clothes are us,
> yet not us. We're more than the cloth
> we wrap ourselves in. Daily we put on
> these shirts and dresses, fill the emptiness
> inside the sleeves and lives we walk around in.
> But there's always a hunger, the questions
> of what it means to belong.

How do these lines connect to a larger theme in the narrative as a whole? What is the central question the book as a whole is trying to address? What poem or lines from a poem identify the heart of the book as a whole?

32.What are some common ways media portrays Italians, such as in television series or movies? Where does the poem reflect or differ from these portrayals?

33. How does the poem "The New Colossus," by Emma Lazarus reflect or echo events or feelings in these narrative poems?

EXTENDED AND RELATED READINGS

Barzini, Luigi. *The Italians*. A Touchstone Book, Simon & Schuster, New York, NY. 1964.

Distasi, Lawrence. *Una Storia Segreta; The Secret History of the Italian American Evacuation and Internment During World War II*. Heyday Books, Berkeley, CA. 2001.

Gambino, Richard. *Blood of My Blood: The Dilemma of the Italian-Americans*. Second edition. Guernica Editions, Tonawanda, NY. 1974.

Gillan, Maria Mazziotti, Gillan, Jennifer. *Unsettling America, an Anthology of Contemporary Multicultural Poetry*. Penguin Books. New York, NY. 1994.

————. *Things My Mother Told Me*. Guernica Editions, Toronto, Canada. 1999.

Hooper, John. *The Italians*. Penguin Random House. New York, NY. 2015.

Laurino, Maria. *Italian Americans*. W.W. Norton & Company, New York, NY. 2015.

Lazarus, Emma. "The New Colossus." The Statue of Liberty National Monument. Accessed Jan. 9, 2019. https://www.nps.gov/stli/learn/historyculture/colossus.htm

Mangione, Jerre. *La Storia: Five Centuries of the Italian American Experience*. Harper Collins. New York, NY. 1992.

Napoli, Donna Jo. *The King of Mulberry Street*. Yearling, a division of Random House, Inc. New York, NY. 1992.

Scarpaci, Vincenza. *The Journey of the Italians in America*. Pelican Publishing House, Singapore. 2008.

Stapinski, Helene. *Murder in Matera: A True Story of Passion, Family, and Forgiveness in Southern Italy*. Dey St., an Imprint of William Morrow, 2018.

BIBLIOGRAPHY

Alioto, Mariano. "Mariano Alioto - Alioto Family History." *Google Sites*, sites.google.com/site/aliotomario/mariano-alioto. Accessed 10 Jan. 2019.

"Anti-Italianism." *Wikipedia, the Free Encyclopedia*, Wikimedia Foundation, Inc,. 8 Jan. 2019, en.wikipedia.org/wiki/Anti-Italianism. Accessed 4 Feb. 2019.

"Barbary Coast, San Francisco." *En.Wikipedia.Org*. 2019. https://en.wikipedia.org/wiki/Barbary_Coast,_San_Francisco. Accessed 10 Jan. 2019.

"Barber." *Wikipedia, the Free Encyclopedia*, Wikimedia Foundation, Inc., 16 Jan. 2019, en.wikipedia.org/wiki/Barber. Accessed 18 Jan. 2019.

"Barbering Timeline - National Barber Museum." *Home - National Barber Museum*, www.nationalbarbermuseum.org/about/barbering-timeline. Accessed 10 19 Jan. 2019.

Barker, Malcolm E. "More San Francisco Memoirs, 1852-1899." *Google Books, Londonborn Publication*, San Francisco,CA,1996. Accessed 13 Jan. 2019.

Barnes, Meritt. "Corruption Central: Peter P. McDonough." *FoundSF*, www.foundsf.org/. Accessed 10 Jan. 2019.

Bean, Walton. "Boss Ruef's San Francisco." *Google Books, University of California, Berkeley*, CA, 1952. books.google.co.in/. Accessed 10 Jan. 2019.

Bencivenni, Marcella. "Italian Immigrant Radical Culture." *Google Books, New York University Press*, 2011. books.google.co.in/books. Accessed 13 Jan. 2019.

"Ben Selvin | Biography & History." *All Music*, www.allmusic.com/artist/ben-selvin-mn0000794156/biography. Accessed 13 Jan. 2019.

"Benito Mussolini Biography - Life, Family, Story, Death, School, Mother, Old, Information, Born, Time, Year." *Notable Biographies*, Encyclopedia of World Biography, www.notablebiographies.com/Mo-Ni/Mussolini-Benito.html. Accessed 13 Jan. 2019.

Bevk, Alex. "A Photo Salute to the Ghosts of San Francisco's Industrial Past." *Curbed SF*, 29 Aug. 2014. sf.curbed.com/2014/8/29/10055494/a-photo-salute-to-the-ghosts-of-san-franciscos-industrial-past. Accessed 13 Jan. 2019.

—————. "For Its 100th Birthday, Looking Back at the Panama-Pacific International Exposition." *Curbed SF*, 18 Feb. 2015. sf.curbed.com/archives/2015/02/18/for_its_100th_birthday_looking_back_at_the_panamapacific_international_exposition.php. Accessed 13 Jan. 2019.

"Black Hand (extortion)." *Wikipedia, the Free Encyclopedia*, Wikimedia Foundation, Inc., 20 Nov. 2018. en.wikipedia.org/wiki/Black_Hand_(extortion). Accessed 11 Jan. 2019.

Black, Jon. "The Black Hand - GangRule." *Gangrule - The History of the Mafia*, 11 Apr. 2014. www.gangrule.com/gangs/the-black-hand. Accessed 10 Jan. 2019.

Blakemore, Erin. "The Grisly Story of America's Largest Lynching." *History.com*, A&E Television Networks, 25 Oct. 2017, www.history.com/news/the-grisly-story-of-americas-largest-lynching. Accessed 10 Jan. 2019.

Branca-Santos, Paula. "Injustice Ignored: The Internment of Italian Americans during World War II." *DigitalCommons@Pace | Pace University Research*, Pace Int'l L. Rev. 151, Apr. 2001.

Bressan, David. "December 28, 1908: The Tsunami of Messina." *Scientific American Blog Network*, 28 Dec. 2012. blogs.scientificamerican.com/history-of-geology/december-28-1908-the-tsunami-of-messina/. Accessed 10 Jan. 2019.

Brown Cross, Ira. "A History Of The Labor Movement In California." *Google Books, University of California Press*, 1935. books.google.co.in/books. Accessed 10 Jan 2019.

Bunker, Kevin. "CPRR Discussion Group - Central Pacific Railroad

Photographic History Museum." *CPRR Discussion Group - Central Pacific Railroad Photographic History Museum*, 17 Feb. 2008. discussion. cprr.net/2008/02/transcontinental-train-trip-in-1923.html. Accessed 13 Jan. 2019.

"Calabrese | Encyclopedia.com." *Encyclopedia.com | Free Online Encyclopedia*, Encyclopedia of World Cultures, The Gale Group. 1996. www. encyclopedia.com/sports-and-everyday-life/food-and-drink/food-and-cooking/calabrese. Accessed 14 Jan. 2019.

"Calabria." *Wikipedia, the Free Encyclopedia*, Wikimedia Foundation, Inc., 30 Dec. 2018. en.wikipedia.org/wiki/Calabria. Accessed 12 Jan. 2019.

"Calabrian Diaspora." *Wikipedia, the Free Encyclopedia*, Wikimedia Foundation, Inc, 16 Nov. 2018, en.wikipedia.org/wiki/Calabrian_diaspora. Accessed 4 Feb. 2019.

"Camorra." *Wikipedia, the Free Encyclopedia*, Wikimedia Foundation, Inc., 27 Nov. 2018. en.wikipedia.org/wiki/Camorra. Accessed 11 Jan. 2019.

Cannato, Vincent. "What Sets Italian Americans Off From Other Immigrants?" *National Endowment for the Humanities (NEH)*, Jan. 2015. www.neh.gov/humanities/2015/januaryfebruary/feature/what-sets-italian-americans-other-immigrants. Accessed 12 Jan. 2019.

"The Cannery." *San Francisco, A History*, 11 May, 2011. sanfranciscohistory. blogspot.com/2011/03/cannery.html. Accessed 10 Jan. 2019.

Caravetta, Francesco. "Paura e Deliro a San Lucido." *Antichi Delitti*, 1 July 2015. cosenzaantichidelitti.blogspot.com/2015/07/paura-e-delirio-san-lucido.html. Accessed 11 Jan. 2019.

Carlsson, Chris. "Abe Ruef and the Union Labor Party." *FoundSF*, www. foundsf.org/index.php?title=Abe_Ruef_and_the_Union_Labor_Party. Accessed 13 Jan. 2019.

Carnevale, Nancy. "A New Language, A New World." *Google Books, Stature of Liberty - Ellis Island Centennial*, 2009. books.google.co.in/books. Accessed 10 Jan 2019.

"Category: North Beach." *FoundSF*, foundsf.org/index. php?title=Category:North_Beach. Accessed 13 Jan. 2019.

Cinel, Dino. *From Italy to San Francisco: The Immigrant Experience.* Stanford UP, 1982.

Colella, Nicola. "Southern Italian Immigration." *ITALIAMERICA - Italian Dual Citizenship*, www.italiamerica.org/id49.htm. Accessed 14 Jan. 2019.

Connell, William J., and Pugligese G. Stanislau. "The Routledge History of Italian Americans." *Google Books*, Routledge, New York, New York, 2018, books.google.com/books. Accessed 4 Feb. 2019.

Costantino, Rosetta, and Janet Fletcher. "My Calabria: Rustic Family Cooking from Italy's Undiscovered South." *Google Books, W.W. Norton and Company*, New York, New York, 2010. books.google.com/books. Accessed 14 Jan. 2019.

Crosby, Rosalind G. "The Italians of Los Angeles, 1900." Onlinelibrary, onlinelibrary.wiley.com/doi/pdf/10.1111/j.2050-411X.1993.tb00080. Accessed 15 Jan. 2019.

"Crystal City (detention facility) | Densho Encyclopedia." *Home | Densho Encyclopedia*, encyclopedia.densho.org/categories/Accessed 11 Jan. 2019. encyclopedia.densho.org/Crystal%20City%20(detention%20 facility)/

"Destination America. When Did They Come? | PBS." *PBS: Public Broadcasting Service*, www.pbs.org/destinationamerica/usim_wn_ noflash_5.html. Accessed 12 Jan. 2019.

De Santis, Vanessa. *Special Collections and University Archives – University Libraries | UMass Amherst*, scua.library.umass.edu/digital/ FLURA_2010-08.pdf. Accessed 14 Jan. 2019.

Dempsey, Candace. "How did Italian-American soldiers feel about fighting in Italy during WW2?" *DigitalCommons@UNO - The Institutional Repository of the University of Nebraska Omaha*, 19 Oct. 2017. digitalcommons.unomaha.edu/cgi/viewcontent.cgi?referer=https://

www.google.com/&httpsredir=1&article=2007&context=srcaf. Accessed 14 Jan. 2019.

Di Napoli, Giovanni. "Around the Web: Why We Are Neo-Bourbons." *Il Regno*, Il Regno, 11 Apr. 2009, ilregno2s.blogspot.co.za/2009/04/why-we-are-neo-bourbons.html. Accessed 14 Jan. 2019.

Dickie, John. "Blood Brotherhoods." *Google Books*, US Public Affairs, New York, New York, 2014. books.google.com/books. Accessed 4 Feb. 2019.

"Did My Family Really Come 'Legally??" *American Immigration Council*, 26 Nov. 2018, www.americanimmigrationcouncil.org/research/did-my-family-really-come-legally-todays-immigration-laws-created-a-new-reality. Accessed 1 Feb. 2019.

DiEdoardo, Christina A. "Lanza's Mob: The Mafia and San Francisco." *Google Books, Prager*, Santa Barbara, CA, 2016. books.google.com/books. Accessed 10 Jan. 2019.

Dillingham, William P. "Occupations of the First and Second Generation of Immigrants in the United States. Fecundity of Immigrant Women." *Google Books, Washington Government Printing Office*, 12 Jan. 1910. books.google.com/books. Accessed 10 Jan. 2019.

Edwards, Bill. "Louis Sidney (Sid) Le Protti." *RagPiano.com*, ragpiano.com/comps/leprotti.shtml. Accessed 13 Jan. 2019.

Eisen, George, and Wiggins, David K. "Ethnicity and Sport in North American History and Culture." *Google Books, Praeger imprint of Greenwood Publishing*, Westport, CT, 1994. books.google.co.in/books. Accessed 10 Jan. 2019.

"Ellis Island Part of Statue of Liberty National Monument (U.S. National Park Service)." *NPS.gov Homepage (U.S. National Park Service)*, 25 Oct. 2018. www.nps.gov/elis/index.htm. Accessed 10 Jan. 2019.

"Enemy Alien Internment Camps." *World War II*, www.gentracer.org/internmentcamplist.html. Accessed 15 Jan. 2019.

Fabio, Michelle. "History of Calabria." Bleeding Espresso, bleedingespresso. com/Calabria/history-of-calabria. Accessed 10 May 2019.

Falco, Maria. "The Internment of Italian Americans During World War II." *Falco's Aerie*, www.falcosaerie.me/The%20Internment%20of%20 Italian%20Americans.pdf. Accessed 15 Jan. 2019.

Fichera, Sebastian. "Italy on the Pacific." *Google Books, Palgrave MacMillan*, New York, NY, 2011. books.google.co.in/. Accessed 12 Jan. 2019.

"Forum: Mothers and Mammismo in the Italian Diaspora." *Centro Altreitalie*, www.altreitalie.it/pubblicazioni/rivista/n-50/articoli/forum-mothers-and-mammismo-in-the-italian-diaspora/forum-mothers-and-mammismo-in-the-italian-diaspora.kl. Accessed 14 Jan. 2019.

Gabaccia, Donna R., and Franca Iacovetta. "Women, Gender, and Transnational Lives." *Google Books, University of Toronto Press*, 2002. books.google.com/books. Accessed 14 Jan. 2019.

Gambino, Richard. *Blood of My Blood: The Dilemma of the Italian- Americans. Google Books, Guernica*, Toronto, 1974. books.google.com/books. Accessed 10 Jan. 2019.

German American Internee Coalition. "Websites of Interest." *German American Internee Coalition*, German American Internee Coalition, gaic.info/resources/websites-of-interest/. Accessed 11 Jan. 2019.

"German and Italian Detainees | Densho Encyclopedia." *Home | Densho Encyclopedia*, encyclopedia.densho.org/German_and_Italian_detainees/. Accessed 15 Jan. 2019.

Gillis, Anna M. "Devastation of 1918: Finding Pockets of Hope in the Great Flu Pandemic." *Pacific Standard*, 6 May 2014, psmag.com/ social-justice/devastation-1918-finding-pockets-hope-great-flu-pandemic-80856. Accessed 14 Jan. 2019.

"Giuseppe Garibaldi." *Wikipedia, the Free Encyclopedia*, Wikimedia Foundation, Inc., 13 Dec. 2018, en.wikipedia.org/wiki/Giuseppe_ Garibaldi. Accessed 12 Jan. 2019.

Gjenvick, Paul K. "Steerage Conditions in 1898 - A First-Hand Account | GG Archives." *Historical Ephemera Archives 1880s - 1950s | GG Archives*, www.gjenvick.com/Steerage/1898-SteerageConditions-APersonalExperience.html. Accessed 12 Jan. 2019.

Glynn, Irial. "Emigration Across the Atlantic: Irish, Italians and Swedes Compared,1800-1950— EGO." *EGO | Europäische Geschichte Online*, ieg-ego.eu/en/threads/europe-on-the-road/economic-migration/ irial-glynn-emigration-across-the-atlantic-irish-italians-and-swedes-compared-1800-1950. Accessed 12 Jan. 2019.

"Golden Gate Park." *Wikipedia, the Free Encyclopedia*, Wikimedia Foundation, Inc., 20 Nov. 2018, en.wikipedia.org/wiki/Golden_ Gate_Park. Accessed 11 Jan. 2019.

Gracyk, Tim. "Ben Selvin." *The Red Hot Jazz Archive*, www.redhotjazz. com/selvin.html. Accessed 13 Jan. 2019.

Guzman, Timothy A. "The New Orleans Eleven: The Untold History of the Lynching of Italians in America." *Global Research*, 8 Mar. 2014. www.globalresearch.ca/the-new-orleans-eleven-the-untold-history-of-the-lynching-of-italians-in-america/5372379. Accessed 11 Jan. 2019.

Hall, Stephen S. "Italian-Americans Coming Into Their Own." *Breaking News, World News & Multimedia - The New York Times*, New York Times Magazine, 15 May 1983. www.nytimes.com/1983/05/15/magazine/ italian-americans-coming-into-their-own.html?pagewanted=all. Accessed 11 Jan. 2019.

Hanson, Prof. David J. Ph.D. "Effects of Prohibition Were a Disaster. Created Rather Than Solved Problems." *Alcohol Problems & Solutions*, 20 Nov. 2018. www.alcoholproblemsandsolutions.org/effects-of-prohibition/. Accessed 14 Jan. 2019.

Harris, Michael. "How WWII Affected America's Minorities." *LA Times,* 13 June 2000, articles.latimes.com/2000/jun/13/news/cl-40272. Book review of *Double Victory, A Multicultural History of America in World War II,* by Ronald Takaki Little, Brown. Accessed 14 Jan. 2019.

Hickman, Kennedy. "Battle of the Bulge: Germany's Last Major Offensive of World War II." *ThoughtCo,* 23 Mar. 2017. https://www.thoughtco. com/battle-of-the-bulge-2361488. Accessed 10 Jan. 2019.

Hing, Bill O. "Defining America: Through Immigration Policy." *Google Books, Temple University Press,* Philadelphia, PA, 2004. books.google. co.in/books. Accessed 12 Jan. 2019.

"History of the Game." *Northern California Handball Association,* www. norcalhandball.org/history. Accessed 11 Jan. 2019.

Humbert, Nelli S. "The Business of Crime: Italians and Syndicate Crime in the United States." *Google Books, University of Chicago Press,* IL, 1976. books.google.com/books. Accessed 10 Jan. 2019.

"'I Laugh, Ho, Ho, at Black Hand,' Caruso Says." The Daily Mirror Los Angeles History, 6 Mar. 2010, Reprinted from March 5, 1920latimesblogs.latimes.com/thedailymirror/2010/03/i-laugh-ho-ho-at-black-hand-caruso-says.html. Accessed 11 Jan. 2019.

"In Cerca di Una Nuova Vita, From Italy to California, Italian Immigration 1850 to today." *Home - Museo Italo Americano,* Home - Museo Italo Americano, San Francisco, museoitaloamericano.org/wp-content/uploads/immigration-booklet-FINAL.pdf. Accessed 14 Jan. 2019.

"Influenza 1918, The Flu in San Francisco | American Experience | PBS." *PBS: Public Broadcasting Service,* www.pbs.org/wgbh/americanexperience/features/influenza-san-francisco/. Accessed 14 Jan. 2019.

"Internment of Italian Americans." *Wikipedia, the Free Encyclopedia,* Wikimedia Foundation, Inc., 5 Jan. 2019. en.wikipedia.org/wiki/Internment_of_Italian_Americans. Accessed 11 Jan. 2019.

"Internment of Japanese Americans," Wikipedia, the Free Encyclopedia, Wikimedia Foundation, Inc., en.wikipedia.org/wiki/Japanese_American_internment. Accessed 4 Oct. 2019.

"Italian Americans | PBS." *Page 1 | Italian Americans | PBS*, www.pbs. org/the-italian-americans/being-italian/1/. Accessed 13 Jan. 2019.

The Italian American Experience. "IAP 48: The Hidden History of Southern Italy's Glory Part Three." *The Italian American Experience*, 3 Sept. 2017. italianamericanexperience.com/hidden-history-southern-italys-glory-part-three/. Accessed 14 Jan. 2019.

Italian American Museum. "Italian American Museum." *Italian American Museum*, www.italianamericanmuseum.org/news/new_echos_of_ellis. html. Accessed 13 Jan. 2019.

"Italian Culture - Family." *Cultural Atlas*, culturalatlas.sbs.com.au/italian-culture/italian-culture-family#italian-culture-family. Accessed 14 Jan. 2019.

"Italian Diaspora." *Wikipedia, the Free Encyclopedia*, Wikimedia Foundation, Inc., "Italian Diaspora." *Wikipedia, the Free Encyclopedia*, Wikimedia Foundation, Inc., 23 Dec. 2018, en.wikipedia.org/wiki/Italian_ diaspora. Accessed 14 Jan. 2019.

"The Italian Emigrants." *YouTube*, 26 Dec. 2007. www.youtube.com/ watch?v=B911djBOwdM. Accessed 12 Jan. 2019.

"Italian Immigrants And Organized Labor." *The Italian Tribune*, 2017. http://www.italiantribune.com/immigrants_labor/. Accessed 10 Jan 2019.

"Italian Immigration." www2.needham.k12.ma.us/nhs/cur/kane98/kane_ p6_immig/italianII/rjs.html. Accessed 14 Jan. 2019.

"Italian Immigration - The Great Italian Diaspora." *The Italian Legacy - Your Guide to All Things Italian*, www.italianlegacy. com/italian-immigration.html. Accessed 14 Jan. 2019.

"Italian - L'Isola Dell Lagrime - Immigration... Classroom Presentation | Teacher Resources - Library of Congress." *Home | Library of Congress*, www.loc.gov/teachers/classroommaterials/presentationsandactivities/ presentations/immigration/italian4.html. Accessed 12 Jan. 2019.

"Italians to America, 1855-1900 | Findmypast.com." *Trace Your Family Tree Online | Genealogy & Ancestry from Findmypast | Findmypast. com*, www.findmypast.com/articles/world-records/full-list-of-united-states-records/immigration-and-travel/italians-to-america-1855-1900. Accessed 13 Jan. 2019.

"Italian Unification." *Wikipedia, the Free Encyclopedia*, Wikimedia Foundation, Inc., 13 Jan. 2019. en.wikipedia.org/wiki/Italian_unification. Accessed 12 Jan. 2019.

James, Marquis, and Bessie James. "The Story of Bank of America." *Google Books, Beard Books*, Washington DC, 1954. books.google.co.in/books. Accessed 13 Jan. 2019.

Jarboe Russlle, Jan. "5 Surprises About America's Imprisoning People During World War II". *Business Insider*, 2015. https://www.businessinsider.com/5-surprises-about-american-internment-during-world-war-ii-2015-1. Accessed 10 Jan 2019.

"Journey to America." *Spartacus Educational*, 20 Jan. 2018. spartacus-educational.com/USAEjourney.htm. Accessed 13 Jan. 2019.

Kamiya, Gary. "S.F. Corruption Machine Humming Along Before, After 1906 Quake." *SFChronicle.com, San Francisco Chronicle*, 10 July 2015. www.sfchronicle.com/politics/article/S-F-corruption-machine-humming-along-before-6378193.php. Accessed 10 Jan. 2019.

————. "SF's Forgotten Jazz Pioneer." *SFChronicle.com*, 29 Sept. 2017. www.sfchronicle.com/bayarea/article/SF-s-forgotten-jazz-pioneer-12242019.php. Accessed 13 Jan. 2019.

————. "When Bombings Menaced A North Beach Church." *SFGate*, 2014. www.sfgate.com/bayarea/article/When-bombings-menaced-a-North-Beach-church-5909850.php. Accessed 10 Jan 2019.

Keshavarz, Shahab. "Italian Internment WWII." *Italian Historical Society of America*, www.italianhistorical.org/page19a.html. Accessed 11 Jan. 2019.

Knight, Robert E. "Industrial Relations in the San Francisco Bay Area,

1900-1918." *Google Books, University of California Press*, Berkeley, CA, 1960. books.google.co.in/books. Accessed 13 Jan. 2019.

Kraut, Alan M. "Immigration, Ethnicity, and the Pandemic." *PubMed Central (PMC)*, www.ncbi.nlm.nih.gov/pmc/articles/PMC2862341/. Accessed 14 Jan. 2019.

Krippner, Stanley, et al. "The Indigenous Healing Tradition in Calabria, Italy." *Digital Commons @ CIIS*, California Institute of Integral Studies, International Journal of Transpersonal Studies, 1 Jan. 2011. digitalcommons.ciis.edu/cgi/viewcontent. cgi?article=1117&context=ijts-transpersonalstudies. Accessed 11 Jan. 2019.

LaGumina, Salvatore J., et al. "The Italian American Experience." *Google Books, Garland Publishing*, New York, NY, 2000. books.google.com/books. Accessed 12 Jan. 2019.

Lang, Arne K. "The Nelson-Wolgast Fight and the San Francisco Boxing Scene, 1900_ŃĐ1914." *Google Books, McFarland and Co. Inc.*, Jefferson, NC, 2012, books.google.co.in/books. Accessed 10 Jan. 2019.

Lee, Laura. "The History of Laundry and Soap Making in Italy." *Digging Up Roots in the Boot*, 12 Apr. 2017, digginguprootsintheboot.com/history-laundry-soap-making-italy/. Accessed 12 Jan. 2019.

Little, Becky. "The Birth of 'Illegal? Immigration." *HISTORY*, 7 Sept. 2017, www.history.com/news/the-birth-of-illegal-immigration. Accessed 4 Feb. 2019.

"March 14, 1891 – Lynching Of Eleven Italian Americans In New Orleans." *Legal Legacy*, 2019. //legallegacy.wordpress.com/2016/03/14/march-14-1891-lynching-of-eleven-italian-americans-in-new-orleans/. Accessed 10 Jan 2019.

Mathews, Jeff. "Recent Eruptions of Mt. Vesuvius & the Fountain of Spina Corona." *Naples Life, Death & Miracle*, 2010. www.naplesldm.com/eruptions.php. Accessed 13 Jan. 2019.

"Messina Earthquake and Tsunami of 1908 | Italy." *Encyclopedia Britannica*, 21 Dec. 2018. www.britannica.com/event/Messina-earthquake-and-tsunami-of-1908. Accessed 10 Jan. 2019.

Molnar, Alexandra. "History of Italian Immigration." *From Europe to America: Immigration Through Family Tales*, 15 Dec. 2010. www.mtholyoke. edu/~molna22a/classweb/politics/Italianhistory.html. Accessed 10 Jan. 2019.

Montagne, Renee. "Remembering the 1906 San Francisco Earthquake." *NPR.org*, NPR, 11 Apr. 2006. www.npr.org/templates/story/story. php?storyId=5334411. Accessed 13 Jan. 2019.

"Naturalization Records." *National Archives*, 22 Aug. 2016, www.archives. gov/research/naturalization/naturalization.html. Accessed 1 Feb. 2019.

"1906 Earthquake: Refugee Camps - Presidio of San Francisco (U.S. National Park Service)." *NPS.gov Homepage (U.S. National Park Service)*, 28 Feb. 2015. www.nps.gov/prsf/learn/historyculture/1906-earthquake-relief-efforts-living-accommodations.htm. Accessed 10 Jan. 2019.

"1906 San Francisco Earthquake." *Wikipedia, the Free Encyclopedia*, Wikimedia Foundation, Inc., en.wikipedia.org/wiki/1906_ San_Francisco_earthquake/. Accessed 10 Jan. 2019.

"1908 Messina Earthquake." *Wikipedia, the Free Encyclopedia*, Wikimedia Foundation, Inc., 2 Jan. 2019, en.wikipedia.org/wiki/1908_Messina_ earthquake. Accessed 10 Jan. 2019.

"The 1908 Messina Earthquake: 100-year Retrospective." *Risk Management Solutions - RMS*, 2008, forms2.rms.com/rs/729-DJX-565/images/ eq_1908_messina_eq.pdf. Accessed 10 Jan. 2019.

Nolte, Carl. "The Great Quake: 1906-2006 / Rising from the Ashes." *SFGate*, 18 Apr. 2006. www.sfgate.com/news/article/The-Great-Quake-1906-2006-Rising-from-the-ashes-2537103.php. Accessed 10 Jan. 2019.

O'Brien, John T., and Marvin Marcus. "Crime and Justice in America." *Google Books, Pergamom Press*, New York, NY, 1979. books.google. co.in/books. Accessed 11 Jan. 2019.

Ong Hing, Bill. "Defining America Through Immigration Policy." *Temple University Press*, Philadelphia, PA, 2004. *Google Books*, https://books. google.co.in/books. Accessed 10 Jan. 2019.

"Organized Crime in Italy." *Wikipedia, the Free Encyclopedia*, Wikimedia Foundation, Inc., 9 Oct. 2018. en.wikipedia.org/wiki/Organized_crime_in_Italy. Accessed 11 Jan. 2019.

"Panama–Pacific International Exposition." *Wikipedia, the Free Encyclopedia*, Wikimedia Foundation, Inc., 10 Jan. 2019. en.wikipedia.org/wiki/Panama%E2%80%93Pacific_International_Exposition. Accessed 13 Jan. 2019.

Panetta, Daniella. "The Role of Italian Women vs. The Role of Italian-American Women." scholarworks.iu.edu/journals/index.php/iusbgender/article/view/13617. Accessed 15 Jan. 2019.

"Pete McDonough." *Wikipedia, the Free Encyclopedia*, Wikimedia Foundation, Inc., 19 Oct. 2018. en.wikipedia.org/wiki/Pete_McDonough. Accessed 10 Jan. 2019.

Petrishen, Brad. "Author Tells of Internment of Italian-Americans in U.S. During WWII." *Telegram.com*, 7 Dec. 2016. www.telegram.com/news/20161207/author-tells-of-internment-of-italian-americans-in-us-during-wwii. Accessed 11 Jan. 2019.

Pozzetta, George. "Italian Americans | Encyclopedia.Com". *Encyclopedia.Com*, 2000, www.encyclopedia.com/history/united-states-and-canada/us-history/italian-americans. Accessed 10 Jan. 2019.

"Progressive Era: 1890–1920s: Effects of 1906 Earthquake | Picture This." *Picture This: California Perspectives on American History*, picturethis. museumca.org/timeline/progressive-era-1890-1920s/effects-1906-earthquake/info. Accessed 10 Jan. 2019.

"Prohibition in the United States." *Wikipedia, the Free Encyclopedia*, Wikimedia Foundation, Inc., 12 Jan. 2019. en.wikipedia.org/wiki/Prohibition_in_the_United_States. Accessed 14 Jan. 2019.

"Prohibition Profits Transformed the Mob." *Prohibition: An Interactive History*, The Mob Museum, prohibition.themobmuseum.org/the-history/the-rise-of-organized-crime/the-mob-during-prohibition/. Accessed 4 Feb. 2019.

"Prohibition: Speakeasies, Loopholes And Politics." *NPR.org*, 10 June 2011. www.npr.org/2011/06/10/137077599/prohibition-speakeasies-loopholes-and-politics. Accessed 14 Jan. 2019.

Rapczynski, Joan. "99.03.06: The Italian Immigrant Experience in America (1870-1920)." *The Yale-New Haven Teachers Institute*, 2018. teachersinstitute.yale.edu/curriculum/units/1999/3/99.03.06.x.html.

"Revisionism of Risorgimento." *Wikipedia, the Free Encyclopedia*, Wikimedia Foundation, Inc., 27 May 2018. en.wikipedia.org/wiki/Revisionism_of_Risorgimento. Accessed 14 Jan. 2019.

"Room Five: Little Italy, San Francisco." *The Bancroft Library | UC Berkeley Library*. bancroft.berkeley.edu/collections/italianamericans/exhibit_room05.html. Accessed 12 Jan. 2019.

S., Nebel, et al. "Ta Chòrta: Wild Edible Greens Used in the Graecanic Area in Calabria, Southern Italy. - PubMed - NCBI." *National Center for Biotechnology Information*, www.ncbi.nlm.nih.gov/pubmed/16843569. Accessed 14 Jan. 2019.

Sakellariou, Eleni. "Southern Italy in the Late Middle Ages." *Google Books, Koninklijke Brill, Leiden*, The Netherlands, 2012. books.google.com/books. Accessed 14 Jan. 2019.

Salerno-Mele, Armando. "The Ancient and Noble Art of Silk." *Madeinitaly For Me*, 11 Jan. 2017, www.madeinitalyfor.me/en/info/lantica-e-nobile-arte-serica/. Accessed 14 Jan. 2019.

"San Francisco, California and the 1918-1919 Influenza Epidemic." *The American Influenza Epidemic of 1918: A Digital Encyclopedia*, University of Michigan Center for the History of Medicine and Michigan Publishing, University of Michigan Library, www.influenzaarchive.org/cities/city-sanfrancisco.html#. Accessed 14 Jan. 2019.

"The San Francisco Earthquake, 1906." *EyeWitness to History - History Through the Eyes of Those Who Lived It*, www.eyewitnesstohistory.com/sfeq.htm. Accessed 10 Jan. 2019.

"San Francisco Graft Trials." *Wikipedia, the Free Encyclopedia*, Wikimedia Foundation, Inc., 22 Dec. 2018. en.wikipedia.org/wiki/San_Francisco_graft_trials. Accessed 10 Jan. 2019.

Sawler, Stephanie. "This Day In History: May 27, 1937 - Hornblower Cruises & Events Blog." *Hornblower Cruises & Events Blog*, Hornblower, 27 May 2014. blog.hornblower.com/2014/05/27/this-day-in-history-may-27-1937/#.Wkc4VyMrI1g. Accessed 10 Jan. 2019.

Scarpaci, Vincenza. "The Journey of the Italians in America." *Google Books, Pelican Publishing Co.*, Singapore, 2008. books.google.co.in/. Accessed 12 Jan. 2019.

Schnabl, Carly. "The Origins of the 'ndrangheta of Calabria: Italy's Most Powerful Mafia | UCL Events." *UCL Blogs - UCL UCL Blogs*, 14 Mar. 2011. blogs.ucl.ac.uk/events/2011/03/14/the-origins-of-the-ndrangheta-of-calabria-italys-most-powerful-mafia/. Accessed 11 Jan. 2019.

"A Science Odyssey: People and Discoveries: Bubonic Plague Hits San Francisco." *PBS: Public Broadcasting Service*, PBS, www.pbs.org/wgbh/aso/databank/entries/dm00bu.html. Accessed 10 Jan. 2019.

Scottoline, Lisa. "The Internment of Italian Americans During WW1-Lisa Scottoline." Lisa Scottoline, https://scottoline.com/internmentexecutive-summary/. Accessed 10 Jan. 2019.

Signore, Luca. "Silenzio: The Effects of World War II Policy on Italian-American Identity." *Scholar Commons | Santa Clara University Research*, 2014. scholarcommons.scu.edu/cgi/viewcontent.cgi?referer=https://www.google.com/&httpsredir=1&article=1013&context=historical-perspectives. Accessed 12 Jan. 2019.

Simons, Cindy. "History Files: Del Monte Cannery." *San Leandro, CA Patch*, Patch, 3 Dec. 2012. patch.com/california/sanleandro/del-monte-cannery-a-san-leandro-institution-for-3-4-o61385d32b1. Accessed 10 Jan. 2019.

Singleton, Kate, and the International Herald Tribune. "ITALIAN FASHION: Many Yarns Spin a Revival in Calabria." *Breaking*

News, World News & Multimedia - The New York Times, 2 Mar. 2001, www.nytimes.com/2001/03/02/news/italian-fashion-many-yarns-spin-a-revival-in-calabria.html. Accessed 14 Jan. 2019.

"Sites of Shame | Densho Encyclopedia." Home | Densho Encyclopedia, densho.org/sitesofshame/map.html. Accessed 18 Feb. 2019.

Sorrentino, Frank M., and Jerome Krase. "The Review of Italian American Studies." *Google Books, Lexington Books*, Lanham, MD, 2000. books.google.co.in/books. Accessed 14 Jan. 2019.

Sours, Omus, and Mark Bishop. "The Face of Death." *Google Books, Trafford Publishing*, Victoria, Canada, 2003. books.google.co.in/books. Accessed 11 Jan. 2019.

"Southern Italy." *Wikipedia, the Free Encyclopedia*, Wikimedia Foundation, Inc, 8 Jan. 2019, en.wikipedia.org/wiki/Southern_Italy. Accessed 17 Jan. 2019.

"Spinning Wool ... The Hard Way!" *Transparent.com Blogs | Transparent Language*, blogs.transparent.com/italian/spinning-wool-the-hard-way/. Accessed 12 Jan. 2019.

"Steerage Definition, Conditions, Immigrant Journey | GG Archives." *Historical Ephemera Archives 1880s - 1950s | GG Archives*, www.gjenvick.com/Steerage/index.html. Accessed 13 Jan. 2019.

Story, Fiona. "Tarantella: An Italian Folk Dance." *Preston Street - Our Little Italy*, www.ottawaitalians.com/Heritage/tarantella.htm. Accessed 14 Jan. 2019.

Tardi, Susanna. The Changing Roles of Italian American Women. In: Connell W.J., Gardaphé F. (eds) Anti-Italianism. (2010) Italian and Italian American Studies. Palgrave Macmillan, New York

Taylor, David. "During World War II, The U.S. Saw Italian-Americans As A Threat To Homeland Security." *Smithsonian*, 2017, www.smithsonianmag.com/history/italian-americans-were-considered-enemy-aliens-world-war-ii-180962021/. Accessed 10 Jan. 2019.

Tetrazzini, Luisa, singer, Moore, Thomas, lyrics. "The Last Rose of Summer." Victor 6343, 17, March, 1911, Camden, New Jersey. http://www. loc.gov/jukebox/recordings/detail/id/2165/. Accessed 17 Jan. 2019

Texas Historical Commission. "Crystal City (Family) Internment Camp | THC.Texas.gov - Texas Historical Commission." *THC. Texas. Gov - Texas Historical Commission*, 20 Dec. 2018. www.thc.texas.gov/ preserve/projects-and-programs/military-history/texas-world-war-ii/ world-war-ii-japanese-american-2. Accessed 11 Jan. 2019.

Tobias, Asti, and Chris Lee. "1908 Messina Earthquake, Italy." *Earthquakes and Volcanoes (Medc's & LEDC's)*, astichris.weebly.com/1908-messina-earthquake-italy.html. Accessed 10 Jan. 2019.

Tonelli, Bill. "Thriller Draws On Oppression Of Italians in Wartime U.S." *Breaking News, World News & Multimedia - The New York Times*, 2 Aug. 2004. www.nytimes.com/2004/08/02/books/thriller-draws-on-oppression-of-italians-in-wartime-us.html. Accessed 11 Jan. 2019.

Trefny, Ben, and Rose Aguilar. "75 Years Later, Bay Area Italian Americans Remember Wartime Restrictions, Internment." *KALW.Org*, 2017. www. kalw.org/post/75-years-later-bay-area-italian-americans-remember-wartime-restrictions-internment#stream/0. Accessed 10 Jan 2019.

Ungaretti, Lori. "Legendary Locals of San Francisco's Richmond, Sunset, and Golden Gate Park." *Google Books*, Arcadia Publishing, Charleston, SC, 2014. books.google.co.in/books. Accessed 10 Jan. 2019.

"Unification of Italian States - Countries." *Office of the Historian*, history. state.gov/countries/issues/italian-unification. Accessed 12 Jan. 2019.

Varzally, Allison. "Making a Non-White America, Californians Coloring Outside Ethnic Lines 1925-1955." *UC California Press* Berkeley and Los Angeles, 2008. content.ucpress.edu/pages/10594/10594.ch01. pdf. Accessed 11 Jan. 2019.

Virtual Museum of San Francisco. "Police Work in the 1920s." *Museum of the City of San Francisco*, Virtual Museum of San Francisco, www. sfmuseum.org/sfpd/sfpd3.html. Accessed 11 Jan. 2019.

Walker, Richard. "San Francisco's Haymarket: A Redemptive Tale of Class Struggle." *FoundSF*, foundsf.org/index.php?title=San_Francisco%E2%80%99s_Haymarket:_A_Redemptive_Tale_of_Class_Struggle. Accessed 10 Jan. 2019.

"Warren G. Harding." *Wikipedia, the Free Encyclopedia*, Wikimedia Foundation, Inc., 11 Jan. 2019, en.wikipedia.org/wiki/Warren_G._Harding. Accessed 10 Jan. 2019.

"Washboards, Boxes and Wash-houses in France, Italy and Spain." *History of Housekeeping, Household Antiques, Domestic Objects*, 23 Jan. 2008. www.oldandinteresting.com/french-washboards.aspx. Accessed 10 Jan. 2019.

"Websites of Interest." *German American Internee Coalition*, gaic.info/resources/websites-of-interest/. Accessed 15 Jan. 2019.

Weisbord, Vera B. "Italian Strikers in Lodi, N.J. 1926." *Marxists Internet Archive*, "La Parola del Popolo," ww.marxists.org/archive/weisbord/Lodi.htm. Accessed 13 Jan. 2019.

"Welcome to Immigration." *Scholastic Publishes Literacy Resources and Children's Books for Kids of All Ages*, teacher.scholastic.com/activities/immigration/tour/stop9.htm. Accessed 4 Feb. 2019.

"What Do I Need To Start Spinning? | Abby's Yarns." *Abby's Yarns | Because One Way or Another, It's All About Yarn*, 28 Aug. 2007, abbysyarns.com/2007/08/what-do-i-need-to-start-spinning/. Accessed 14 Jan. 2019.

"When Bombings Menaced A North Beach Church." *SFGate*, 2019. https://www.sfgate.com/bayarea/article/When-bombings-menaced-a-North-Beach-church-%205909850.php. Accessed 10 Jan. 2019.

Wirth, Christa. "Memories of Belonging: Descendants of Italian Migrants to the United States, 1884-Present." *Google Books, Koniklijke Brill Publishing*, 2015, books.google.co.in/books. Accessed 12 Jan. 2019.

Wolf, Christopher. "A Brief History Of America's Hostility To A Previous
Generation Of Mediterranean Migrants — Italians." *Public Radio
International*, 2015. https://www.pri.org/stories/2015-11-26/brief-
history-america-s-hostility-previous-generation-mediterranean-
migrants. Accessed 10 Jan. 2019.

Yollin, Patricia. "A SECRET HISTORY / The Harassment Of Italians
During World War II Has Particular Relevance Today And Serves
As A Warning Of What Could Happen." *SFGate*, 2001, https://
www.sfgate.com/magazine/article/A-SECRET-HISTORY-The-
harassment-of-Italians-2866287.php. Accessed 10 Jan. 2019.

ACKNOWLEDGMENTS

Grateful recognition is given to these literary periodicals in which the following poems originally appeared:

Paterson Literary Review, "Gaetano Learns from a Stranger"
Evening Street Press, "Luisa's Story," "The Cut, Gaetano's Fear,"
  "Luisa Explains How it Happened, "The Way it Was, Gaetano's
  Prayer," "Gaetano's Dream," and "Luisa Alone"

My sincere appreciation and deep gratitude to Michael Citrino, Maria Mazziotti Gillan, Michael Newell, Nicholas Samaras, and Sharman Murphy for their ongoing support and belief in my work. Thank you to Virginia and Neil Olson for their inspiring love of Italy and the insights they've shared, and to Greg Clinton whose suggestion to listen to Fauré's, *Après un rêve*, (Op. 7, No. 1), started me on the journey that unfolded into this manuscript.

ABOUT THE AUTHOR

ANNA CITRINO grew up in California and taught abroad in international schools for twenty-six years in six different countries: Turkey, Kuwait, Singapore, Saudi Arabia, India, and the United Kingdom. Her current home is Soquel, California. A graduate of the Bread Loaf School of English in Vermont, Citrino's work has appeared in various literary journals including, *The Adirondack Review*, *Bellowing Ark*, *Canary*, *Evening Street Review*, *Paterson Literary Review*, *phren-z*, and *Spillway*, among other publications. She has also published two chapbooks, *Saudade*, and *To Find a River*. Read more of Anna's writing at annacitrino.com.

VIA FOLIOS

A refereed book series dedicated to the culture of Italians and Italian Americans.

MARIA FAMÀ. *The Good for the Good*. Vol. 143. Poetry. $8
ROSEMARY CAPPELLO. *Wonderful Disaster*. Vol. 142. Poetry. $14
B. AMORE. *Journeys on the Wheel*. Vol. 141. Poetry. $14
ALDO PALAZZESCHI. *The Manifestos of Aldo Palazzeschi*. Vol 140. Literature. $14
ROSS TALARICO. *The Reckoning*. Vol 139. Poetry. $24
MICHELLE REALE. *Season of Subtraction*. Vol 138. Poetry. $8
MARISA FRASCA. *Wild Fennel*. Vol 137. Poetry. $10
RITA ESPOSITO WATSON. *Italian Kisses*. Vol. 136. Memoir. $14
SARA FRUNER. *Bitter Bites from Sugar Hills*. Vol. 135. Poetry. $12
KATHY CURTO. *Not for Nothing*. Vol. 134. Memoir. $16
JENNIFER MARTELLI. *My Tarantella*. Vol. 133. Poetry. $10
MARIA TERRONE. *At Home in the New World*. Vol. 132. Essays. $16
GIL FAGIANI. *Missing Madonnas*. Vol. 131. Poetry. $14
LEWIS TURCO. *The Sonnetarium*. Vol. 130. Poetry. $12
JOE AMATO. *Samuel Taylor's Hollywood Adventure*. Vol. 129. Novel. $20
BEA TUSIANI. *Con Amore*. Vol. 128. Memoir. $16
MARIA GIURA. *What My Father Taught Me*. Vol. 127. Poetry. $12
STANISLAO PUGLIESE. *A Century of Sinatra*. Vol. 126. Popular Culture. $12
TONY ARDIZZONE. *The Arab's Ox*. Vol. 125. Novel. $18
PHYLLIS CAPELLO. *Packs Small Plays Big*. Vol. 124. Literature.
FRED GARDAPHÉ. *Read 'em and Reap*. Vol. 123. Criticism. $22
JOSEPH A. AMATO. *Diagnostics*. Vol 122. Literature. $12.
DENNIS BARONE. *Second Thoughts*. Vol 121. Poetry. $10
OLIVIA K. CERRONE. *The Hunger Saint*. Vol 120. Novella. $12
GARIBLADI M. LAPOLLA. *Miss Rollins in Love*. Vol 119. Novel. $24
JOSEPH TUSIANI. *A Clarion Call*. Vol 118. Poetry. $16
JOSEPH A. AMATO. *My Three Sicilies*. Vol 117. Poetry & Prose. $17
MARGHERITA COSTA. *Voice of a Virtuosa and Coutesan*. Vol 116. Poetry. $24
NICOLE SANTALUCIA. *Because I Did Not Die*. Vol 115. Poetry. $12
MARK CIABATTARI. *Preludes to History*. Vol 114. Poetry. $12
HELEN BAROLINI. *Visits*. Vol 113. Novel. $22
ERNESTO LIVORNI. *The Fathers' America*. Vol 112. Poetry. $14
MARIO B. MIGNONE. *The Story of My People*. Vol 111. Non-fiction. $17
GEORGE GUIDA. *The Sleeping Gulf*. Vol 110. Poetry. $14
JOEY NICOLETTI. *Reverse Graffiti*. Vol 109. Poetry. $14
GIOSE RIMANELLI. *Il mestiere del furbo*. Vol 108. Criticism. $20
LEWIS TURCO. *The Hero Enkidu*. Vol 107. Poetry. $14

AL TACCONELLI. *Perhaps Fly*. Vol 106. Poetry. $14

RACHEL GUIDO DEVRIES. *A Woman Unknown in Her Bones*. Vol 105. Poetry. $11

BERNARD BRUNO. *A Tear and a Tear in My Heart*. Vol 104. Non-fiction. $20

FELIX STEFANILE. *Songs of the Sparrow*. Vol 103. Poetry. $30

FRANK POLIZZI. *A New Life with Bianca*. Vol 102. Poetry. $10

GIL FAGIANI. *Stone Walls*. Vol 101. Poetry. $14

LOUISE DESALVO. *Casting Off*. Vol 100. Fiction. $22

MARY JO BONA. *I Stop Waiting for You*. Vol 99. Poetry. $12

RACHEL GUIDO DEVRIES. *Stati zitt, Josie*. Vol 98. Children's Literature. $8

GRACE CAVALIERI. *The Mandate of Heaven*. Vol 97. Poetry. $14

MARISA FRASCA. *Via incanto*. Vol 96. Poetry. $12

DOUGLAS GLADSTONE. *Carving a Niche for Himself*. Vol 95. History. $12

MARIA TERRONE. *Eye to Eye*. Vol 94. Poetry. $14

CONSTANCE SANCETTA. *Here in Cerchio*. Vol 93. Local History. $15

MARIA MAZZIOTTI GILLAN. *Ancestors' Song*. Vol 92. Poetry. $14

MICHAEL PARENTI. *Waiting for Yesterday: Pages from a Street Kid's Life*. Vol 90. Memoir. $15

ANNIE LANZILLOTTO. *Schistsong*. Vol 89. Poetry. $15

EMANUEL DI PASQUALE. *Love Lines*. Vol 88. Poetry. $10

CAROSONE & LOGIUDICE. *Our Naked Lives*. Vol 87. Essays. $15

JAMES PERICONI. *Strangers in a Strange Land: A Survey of Italian-Language American Books*.Vol 86. Book History. $24

DANIELA GIOSEFFI. *Escaping La Vita Della Cucina*. Vol 85. Essays. $22

MARIA FAMÀ. *Mystics in the Family*. Vol 84. Poetry. $10

ROSSANA DEL ZIO. *From Bread and Tomatoes to Zuppa di Pesce "Ciambotto"*.Vol. 83. $15

LORENZO DELBOCA. *Polentoni*. Vol 82. Italian Studies. $15

SAMUEL GHELLI. *A Reference Grammar*. Vol 81. Italian Language. $36

ROSS TALARICO. *Sled Run*. Vol 80. Fiction. $15

FRED MISURELLA. *Only Sons*. Vol 79. Fiction. $14

FRANK LENTRICCHIA. *The Portable Lentricchia*. Vol 78. Fiction. $16

RICHARD VETERE. *The Other Colors in a Snow Storm*. Vol 77. Poetry. $10

GARIBALDI LAPOLLA. *Fire in the Flesh*. Vol 76 Fiction & Criticism. $25

GEORGE GUIDA. *The Pope Stories*. Vol 75 Prose. $15

ROBERT VISCUSI. *Ellis Island*. Vol 74. Poetry. $28

ELENA GIANINI BELOTTI. *The Bitter Taste of Strangers Bread*. Vol 73. Fiction. $24

PINO APRILE. *Terroni*. Vol 72. Italian Studies. $20

EMANUEL DI PASQUALE. *Harvest*. Vol 71. Poetry. $10

ROBERT ZWEIG. *Return to Naples*. Vol 70. Memoir. $16

AIROS & CAPPELLI. *Guido*. Vol 69. Italian/American Studies. $12

FRED GARDAPHÉ. *Moustache Pete is Dead! Long Live Moustache Pete!.* Vol 67. Literature/Oral History. $12

PAOLO RUFFILLI. *Dark Room/Camera oscura.* Vol 66. Poetry. $11

HELEN BAROLINI. *Crossing the Alps.* Vol 65. Fiction. $14

COSMO FERRARA. *Profiles of Italian Americans.* Vol 64. Italian Americana. $16

GIL FAGIANI. *Chianti in Connecticut.* Vol 63. Poetry. $10

BASSETTI & D'ACQUINO. *Italic Lessons.* Vol 62. Italian/American Studies. $10

CAVALIERI & PASCARELLI, Eds. *The Poet's Cookbook.* Vol 61. Poetry/Recipes. $12

EMANUEL DI PASQUALE. *Siciliana.* Vol 60. Poetry. $8

NATALIA COSTA, Ed. *Bufalini.* Vol 59. Poetry. $18.

RICHARD VETERE. *Baroque.* Vol 58. Fiction. $18.

LEWIS TURCO. *La Famiglia/The Family.* Vol 57. Memoir. $15

NICK JAMES MILETI. *The Unscrupulous.* Vol 56. Humanities. $20

BASSETTI. ACCOLLA. D'AQUINO. *Italici: An Encounter with Piero Bassetti.* Vol 55. Italian Studies. $8

GIOSE RIMANELLI. *The Three-legged One.* Vol 54. Fiction. $15

CHARLES KLOPP. *Bele Antiche Stòrie.* Vol 53. Criticism. $25

JOSEPH RICAPITO. *Second Wave.* Vol 52. Poetry. $12

GARY MORMINO. *Italians in Florida.* Vol 51. History. $15

GIANFRANCO ANGELUCCI. *Federico F.* Vol 50. Fiction. $15

ANTHONY VALERIO. *The Little Sailor.* Vol 49. Memoir. $9

ROSS TALARICO. *The Reptilian Interludes.* Vol 48. Poetry. $15

RACHEL GUIDO DE VRIES. *Teeny Tiny Tino's Fishing Story.* Vol 47. Children's Literature. $6

EMANUEL DI PASQUALE. *Writing Anew.* Vol 46. Poetry. $15

MARIA FAMÀ. *Looking For Cover.* Vol 45. Poetry. $12

ANTHONY VALERIO. *Toni Cade Bambara's One Sicilian Night.* Vol 44. Poetry. $10

EMANUEL CARNEVALI. *Furnished Rooms.* Vol 43. Poetry. $14

BRENT ADKINS. et al., Ed. *Shifting Borders. Negotiating Places.* Vol 42. Conference. $18

GEORGE GUIDA. *Low Italian.* Vol 41. Poetry. $11

GARDAPHÈ, GIORDANO, TAMBURRI. *Introducing Italian Americana.* Vol 40. Italian/American Studies. $10

DANIELA GIOSEFFI. *Blood Autumn/Autunno di sangue.* Vol 39. Poetry. $15/$25

FRED MISURELLA. *Lies to Live By.* Vol 38. Stories. $15

STEVEN BELLUSCIO. *Constructing a Bibliography.* Vol 37. Italian Americana. $15

ANTHONY JULIAN TAMBURRI, Ed. *Italian Cultural Studies 2002.* Vol 36. Essays. $18

BEA TUSIANI. *con amore.* Vol 35. Memoir. $19

FLAVIA BRIZIO-SKOV, Ed. *Reconstructing Societies in the Aftermath of War.* Vol 34. History. $30

TAMBURRI. et al., Eds. *Italian Cultural Studies 2001*. Vol 33. Essays. $18

ELIZABETH G. MESSINA, Ed. *In Our Own Voices*. Vol 32. Italian/
American Studies. $25

STANISLAO G. PUGLIESE. *Desperate Inscriptions*. Vol 31. History. $12

HOSTERT & TAMBURRI, Eds. *Screening Ethnicity*. Vol 30. Italian/
American Culture. $25

G. PARATI & B. LAWTON, Eds. *Italian Cultural Studies*. Vol 29. Essays. $18

HELEN BAROLINI. *More Italian Hours*. Vol 28. Fiction. $16

FRANCO NASI, Ed. *Intorno alla Via Emilia*. Vol 27. Culture. $16

ARTHUR L. CLEMENTS. *The Book of Madness & Love*. Vol 26. Poetry. $10

JOHN CASEY, et al. *Imagining Humanity*. Vol 25. Interdisciplinary Studies. $18

ROBERT LIMA. *Sardinia/Sardegna*. Vol 24. Poetry. $10

DANIELA GIOSEFFI. *Going On*. Vol 23. Poetry. $10

ROSS TALARICO. *The Journey Home*. Vol 22. Poetry. $12

EMANUEL DI PASQUALE. *The Silver Lake Love Poems*. Vol 21. Poetry. $7

JOSEPH TUSIANI. *Ethnicity*. Vol 20. Poetry. $12

JENNIFER LAGIER. *Second Class Citizen*. Vol 19. Poetry. $8

FELIX STEFANILE. *The Country of Absence*. Vol 18. Poetry. $9

PHILIP CANNISTRARO. *Blackshirts*. Vol 17. History. $12

LUIGI RUSTICHELLI, Ed. *Seminario sul racconto*. Vol 16. Narrative. $10

LEWIS TURCO. *Shaking the Family Tree*. Vol 15. Memoirs. $9

LUIGI RUSTICHELLI, Ed. *Seminario sulla drammaturgia*. Vol 14. Theater/
Essays. $10

FRED GARDAPHÈ. *Moustache Pete is Dead! Long Live Moustache Pete!*. Vol
13. Oral Literature. $10

JONE GAILLARD CORSI. *Il libretto d'autore. 1860 – 1930*. Vol 12. Criticism. $17

HELEN BAROLINI. *Chiaroscuro: Essays of Identity*. Vol 11. Essays. $15

PICARAZZI & FEINSTEIN, Eds. *An African Harlequin in Milan*. Vol 10.
Theater/Essays. $15

JOSEPH RICAPITO. *Florentine Streets & Other Poems*. Vol 9. Poetry. $9

FRED MISURELLA. *Short Time*. Vol 8. Novella. $7

NED CONDINI. *Quartettsatz*. Vol 7. Poetry. $7

ANTHONY JULIAN TAMBURRI, Ed. *Fuori: Essays by Italian/American
Lesbiansand Gays*. Vol 6. Essays. $10

ANTONIO GRAMSCI. P. Verdicchio. Trans. & Intro. *The Southern Question*.
Vol 5.Social Criticism. $5

DANIELA GIOSEFFI. *Word Wounds & Water Flowers*. Vol 4. Poetry. $8

WILEY FEINSTEIN. *Humility's Deceit: Calvino Reading Ariosto Reading
Calvino*. Vol 3. Criticism. $10

PAOLO A. GIORDANO, Ed. *Joseph Tusiani: Poet. Translator. Humanist*. Vol 2.
Criticism. $25

ROBERT VISCUSI. *Oration Upon the Most Recent Death of Christopher
Columbus*. Vol 1. Poetry.

CPSIA information can be obtained
at www.ICGtesting.com
Printed in the USA
BVHW031935110820
586134BV00001B/121